Rochdale
Corporation
Transport

Colin Reeve

ROCHDALE

The town of Rochdale lies eleven miles north of Manchester in the valley of the River Roch. Although mentioned in the Domesday Book, then known as Recedham and possessing a Parish Church dating back to 1194, Rochdale did not achieve prominence until the Industrial Revolution when the town became an important centre for cotton spinning and associated engineering industries. By the end of the nineteenth century Rochdale was said to be the third largest mill town in Lancashire after Bolton and Oldham. It possesses one of the finest Town Halls in the country, designed by WH Crosland along the lines of a Flemish Cloth Hall and bordered on three sides by parks and gardens.

Rochdale is known world wide as the birthplace of the Co-operative movement. It became a Borough in 1856; a County Borough in 1889 and in 1974 a Metropolitan Borough, within the then Metropolitan County of Greater Manchester, absorbing the ring of small towns around it, which had always looked to Rochdale for their services. It is now a Unitary Authority with a population of some 211,000.

With its booming industry and growing population, transport was always important to Rochdale. Ancient tracks cross the moors, notably the 'Roman Road' over Blackstone Edge into Yorkshire and the Limersgate high above the Whitworth valley that for centuries were packhorse routes following the high ground to avoid the swampy, wooded valley bottoms. The first turnpike roads, to Manchester and Burnley, were opened in 1754 followed by the routes to Edenfield and from Littleborough to Halifax and through the Calder Valley to Todmorden.

Linking Lancashire and Yorkshire, the Rochdale Canal was opened between Littleborough and Sowerby Bridge through the Summit Pass in 1798 and on to Manchester via Rochdale six years later. At Summit Top Lock it reached a height of 600 feet above sea level. A branch from Castleton to Heywood was opened in 1834. Although built primarily to carry freight, mainly woollen and cotton goods and coal, a passenger service was operated for a number of years until competition from the adjacent railway brought it to an end.

The Manchester and Leeds Railway reached Rochdale from Manchester in June 1839 and the Summit tunnel was opened two years later. At 2,885 yards it was claimed to be the longest tunnel in the world at the time and cost 41 lives during its construction. Over the next few years branches were opened to Oldham, Bacup and Bury and left a legacy of low bridges in the area that restricted much of the tram and early bus routes to single deck operation.

The Bacup Omnibus Conveyance and Livery Stable Company's horse bus. (BLHM)

A horse bus stands outside the Brown Cow Public House in Norden Village about the turn of the century. (MMT)

EARLY DAYS

The motorbus came late to Rochdale, the first vehicles appearing in the town centre in 1924. However, passenger transport on the roads of the area goes back much further. As long ago as 1772 there was a regular horse-drawn coach service between Manchester and Leeds via Rochdale and Halifax taking nine hours for the journey and in 1777 a coach linked Rochdale with London, taking five days of backbreaking travel to reach the capital. In 1790 a local coach known as the 'Highflyer' was running to Manchester and by 1824 a Royal Mail coach ran nightly between Manchester and York, calling at Rochdale on the way. Another coach, the 'Neptune', ran to Liverpool via Bolton and Wigan.

By the 1860s several horse buses were operating between various town centre hostelries and the outlying districts, the earliest being a short-lived service to Oldham, which commenced in 1861. Five years later the comprehensively named Bacup Omnibus Conveyance and Livery Stable Company Limited of Pippin Bank, Bacup started running a service between Bacup and the Spread Eagle Hotel in Cheetham Street. A timetable dated 1st July 1879 shows four journeys between Bacup and Rochdale and two between Bacup and Facit on Mondays to Fridays and five journeys to Rochdale on Saturdays. There was no Sunday service. There were also other routes from the Roebuck Inn on Yorkshire Street to Heywood and Bury and from the White Hart Hotel, St Mary's Gate to Norden and to Littleborough. Most succumbed to competition from the steam trams, but the Norden route survived until June 1902 when the electric trams started running, most of the employees being retained by the Corporation. The three Norden Company's buses are recorded as having cost 160 guineas each when originally built, but when they were sold at auction in June 1902 they fetched £2 15s 0d, £4 15s 0d and £8 10s 0d respectively.

THE STEAM TRAMWAY

Although horse trams operated in other towns within the Manchester conurbation, they never reached Rochdale, but in 1881 the Manchester, Bury, Rochdale and Oldham Steam Tramways Company was formed as part of a much larger scheme for a network of steam tramways across south east Lancashire. The complicated tale of the ups, but mostly downs of this organisation has been told in great detail in WGS Hyde's excellent book on the subject, but it needs to be mentioned here as it forms an important link in the chain of events leading up to the present day.

The steam tramway was authorised by the Rochdale Tramways Order 1881 and construction began on 27th July the following year when Councillor Tweedale, the Chairman of the Paving Committee, dug up two stone setts at the junction of Oldham Road and Drake Street. A depot was built on Entwisle Road to house the rolling stock on the site of what is now the Central Leisure Centre. The company commenced operations in the Borough on 7th May 1883 with services from the Wellington Hotel in the town centre along Oldham Road to Buersil and to Littleborough via Halifax Road and Smallbridge. They worked as one long through route due to the difficulty of turning steam trams in the town centre. Within two years the lines had reached Healey (1st November 1883), Heywood and Bury (30th May 1884), Whitworth (11th July 1884) and Royton (1st March 1885) but through running to Oldham was prevented by Rochdale Council's insistence that the lines in the town should be to the narrow 3ft 6in gauge, instead of the standard 4ft 8½in gauge used elsewhere.

The company eventually became the second largest steam tramway in Britain, running 91 locomotives and 81 trailers on 30 miles of route. Both engines and passenger cars were smartly painted in brown with black and white lining, although this deteriorated rapidly with the effect of smoke, neglect and the Lancashire weather.

The story of the steam tramway was one of cost cutting and financial chicanery, which resulted in the rapid deterioration of the track and rolling stock. So much so that, in 1884 the Institution of Civil Engineers quoted the state of the company as an example of what could result from building a tramway on the cheap. Four years later it went bankrupt and the network was taken over by a similarly named company omitting Manchester from its title. However, things got no better and on 29th March 1899 Rochdale Council, having conducted a study into the various alternative forms of traction, resolved to give notice of its intention under the Rochdale Corporation Act of that year to take over the track and operate its own electric services when the company's lease expired in 1902, although the notice was not served until December 1902.

The last steam tram route was that to Littleborough which was converted to electric traction in 1905.

ELECTRIC TRAMS

Meanwhile, planning had started on proposals for an extended tramway network. To oversee this the Council created a sub-committee of the Paving Committee which decided that the network should be constructed to the standard 4ft 8½in gauge, the existing steam tramway lines should be rebuilt and new routes added along Bury Road, Edenfield Road, Rooley Moor Road and Milnrow Road as far as the Borough boundaries, as well as a loop serving the railway station. Over the next few years the surrounding Urban Districts of Heywood, Norden, Whitworth, Bacup, Wardle, Littleborough and Milnrow would all obtain powers to build and operate tramways in their areas but, with the exception of Heywood, all leased the tracks to Rochdale, generally for a period of 21 years. Arrangements for depreciation and renewal varied and were to cause problems when the leases became due to expire. Heywood did not lease their tracks, but instead operated the route jointly with Rochdale, taking their share of the revenue and paying their share of the costs, although Rochdale supplied all the cars. The Borough Electrical Engineer, Mr CC Atchison took charge of the planning, construction and initial operation of the tramways.

Having chosen electric traction as its preferred option, the sub-committee now turned its attention to the type of vehicle best suited to run the services. In February 1901 it visited various manufacturers and eventually invited tenders for one example each to six different specifications.

A steam tram leaves the Wellington Hotel at the bottom of Drake Street for Buersil. *(RLS)*

Track construction under way at Spotland Bridge in 1901. Mellor Street comes in from the left and Spotland Road from the right. In the background the tracks divide again, left to Norden via Edenfield Road and right to Spotland via Rooley Moor Road. *(RLS)*

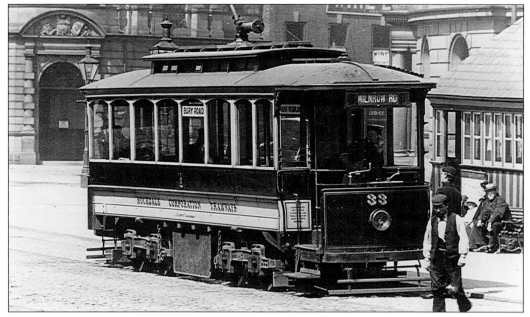

Number 33, a Brush single-truck tram of 1905, stands at the tramway centre while working across town from the Cemetery to Firgrove. *(STA)*

The resultant orders were split equally between the Electric Railway and Tramway Carriage Works Ltd of Preston, the forerunners of English Electric (1-3) and George Milnes and Company of Birkenhead (4-6) all six arriving in 1902.

Numbers 1 and 2 were bogie cars on Brill 22E Maximum Traction trucks with electrical equipment by Dick Kerr, also of Preston, the first being a single-deck combination car and the second an open top double-decker but car number 3, a shorter double-decker, was built on a single Brill 21E truck. The Milnes cars were all bogie double-deckers on different types of Brush trucks with traction motors from the General Electric Company of Schenectady, USA and controllers from British Thomson-Houston of Rugby.

The first route, the short shuttle from the corner of Manchester Road and Dane Street along Bridge Street and Bury Road to the boundary with the Norden Urban District at the Cemetery, opened on 22nd May 1902. For some time the trams were unable to get any nearer to the town centre due to the existing narrow gauge tracks of the steam tramway along the Esplanade, which were still in use, and it was not until July 1904 that the service could be extended to a new terminus in The Butts. In the meantime, a small temporary depot was provided at the bottom of Bury Road.

The lines to Norden and Spotland followed

quickly, commencing on 19th June 1902 and 21st July 1902 respectively. Both services started from a temporary terminus on Blackwater Street and travelled via Spotland Road to Spotland Bridge before diverging, the former following Edenfield Road to Norden and the latter running up Rooley Moor Road as far as Spotland Fold. This arrangement continued until Mellor Street, the new road joining Bury Road and Spotland Bridge, was completed and until then another temporary depot for the two services was provided at Bridgefold. Three more cars, (7-9) were ordered to the same design as number 3, arriving later in the year and allowing the frequencies to be increased.

In September 1903 the Council finally authorised the purchase of the steam tramway company and its conversion to electric traction and negotiations commenced on the price. At the same time work began on covering the River Roch in the town centre creating a wide road known as the Broadway, in the centre of which was to be built the Tramway Centre, a large island containing an office for the inspector, a parcels office and waiting rooms around which the trams would circulate. Work also started on constructing Mellor Street and the new tramway depot, head office and workshops.

In anticipation of the purchase of the steam tramway company and with work due to start on the conversion of its routes, a further ten cars, to the now standard single-truck double-deck design, were ordered from the Brush Electrical Engineering Company of Loughborough, arriving later in the year and numbered 10-19.

In July 1904 a separate Tramways Department was set up independent of the Borough Engineer, and Mr JSD Moffett was appointed the first General Manager of the undertaking. Mr George Webster, the Traffic Manager of the steam tramway company was appointed to a similar post with the Corporation. Mr Webster was to succeed Mr Moffett as General Manager in 1913. At the same time Mellor Street was opened, standard gauge tracks were completed along the Esplanade to the new Tramway Centre and the Bury Road and Norden trams were extended into the town centre. The following month the Mellor Street depot was opened and the Station Circular service started, running one-way via Drake Street, Oldham Road, High Level Road, Tweedale Street and Manchester Road and back along Drake Street to the town centre.

Negotiations on the purchase of the steam tramway company by Manchester, Oldham and Rochdale Corporations dragged on. Agreement could not be reached on the price and the matter went to arbitration. Eventually, a provisional sum of £159,075 was agreed but further costs eventually brought it up to £162,675, Rochdale's share being £70,790. The sale was completed on 13th October 1904. Now, with the steam tramways finally purchased, the Council could go ahead with their assimilation into the network. Work had been going on for some time and things moved rapidly to a conclusion. On 2nd September 1904 the Oldham Road route was re-opened as far as Kings Road and a month later on 5th October it was extended to the Summit Inn at Thornham, the boundary with Royton Urban District. On the same day electric trams took over the former steam service to Marland on the Heywood route and began running along Milnrow Road as far as Newbold Street. On 1st November Oldham Corporation Tramways began operating on the Royton to Thornham section and soon after through services commenced between Hathershaw and Norden, avoiding the need for trams to turn back in the centres of both Oldham and Rochdale. The service was jointly operated by the two Corporations and resulted in Oldham trams appearing in the then rural village of Norden.

On 23rd November 1904 the Facit route was converted as far as the boundary with Whitworth Urban District, just short of Healey Corner at what would later become the site of the Oxford loop, adjacent to the Oxford public house, which today has a picture of a tram as its inn sign, although it is doubtful if many of its patrons know of its significance. Rochdale and Whitworth could not agree on the replacement of the steam trams through Whitworth and it would be nearly six years before Rochdale's electric trams ran beyond Healey Corner. This led to some animosity between the two authorities that was to last well into the motorbus era.

On 26th January 1905 the section of the Littleborough route from Cheetham Street along Yorkshire Street as far as Heybrook Corner was converted and linked to the Spotland service, which was still starting from a temporary terminus on Cheetham Street. Steam trams continued to run to Littleborough via Entwisle Road until 11th May, the route being operated by the Corporation's electric cars from 29th May. The short extension from Littleborough up to the Summit Inn was opened on 12th August and the steam trams were no more. The Entwisle Road depot was demolished and all the remaining rolling stock and redundant equipment was sold. On 20th December the Marland service was extended to Heywood, jointly with Heywood Corporation although Rochdale provided all the cars.

To complete the initial network and to allow a reasonable number of maintenance spares, a further forty cars were delivered, all from Brush. These were ten more single-truck double-deckers (20-29), fourteen bogie single-deckers (30-43) and six bogie double-deckers (44-49), all in 1905 and a further ten bogie single-deckers (50-59) in 1906. The network was now to remain stable for some time although the construction of new lines along John Street and Newgate allowed the Halifax Road, Whitworth Road and Spotland services to reach the Tramway Centre.

The Healey service was eventually extended to Hall Street, Whitworth on 14th June 1910, Facit (20th July 1910), Shawforth (6th September 1910) and finally to Bacup (25th July 1911), this latter section being authorised under a Light Railway Order instead of the more usual Act of Parliament. A small depot was built at Britannia on the boundary between Whitworth and Bacup.

The extensions of the Firgrove service to Milnrow (12th December 1911) and Newhay (1st March 1912) were to be the last changes for a number of years. Ten more single-deck bogie cars (60-69) were purchased from Brush, the last combination type cars to be added to the fleet. At the same time a works car was purchased, fitted for rail grinding and welding, track watering and sanding and a snowplough for the winter.

Traffic continued to grow and in 1920 the first covered top double-deck cars were delivered. These were ten open balcony cars (70-79) from the English Electric Company of Preston to increase service frequencies across the network.

On 9th August 1925, the final link was completed when the Middleton Electric Traction Company's lease expired; Rochdale, Manchester and Oldham Corporations took over its assets, and through operation commenced between Rochdale and Manchester. As Rochdale's share of the purchase of the company five open-top Brush tramcars were acquired. They became 2, 12-15, these numbers having been vacated by withdrawn Rochdale trams. A further ten fully enclosed cars (80-89) were obtained from English Electric mainly to cover for the withdrawal of earlier cars, many of which were becoming more and more unreliable, followed over the next couple of years by five more similar cars (90-94) for the Manchester route. The last two were built in the Corporation's own workshops with Brill trucks

and electrical equipment from the Metropolitan-Vickers Electrical Company of Trafford Park, the only examples of this maker's equipment in the fleet. These were Rochdale's last new cars as tramway abandonment was soon to commence and the whole tramway network would be gone by 1932.

To reduce turning manoeuvres around the Tramway Centre, most services were linked in various different pairings over the years, but after the network reached its maximum extent with the acquisition of the Middleton Company in 1925 the following services were operated.

Bury Road to Newhay
Norden to Thornham
Spotland to Sudden
Station Circular
Rochdale to Littleborough
Littleborough to Summit
Rochdale to Bury via Heywood
Rochdale to Bacup
Rochdale to Manchester via Middleton

Open top double-deckers were necessary to pass under some of the bridges on the system, but were obviously unpopular in the wet weather that was only too prevalent in Rochdale, so in 1930 top covers were fitted to eleven cars, but with withdrawals already in progress no more were so treated.

Rochdale's tramcars were painted in a dignified brown and rich cream livery, which was also to apply to the buses until the 1930s.

1905 Brush bogie car 49 is pictured travelling into town along the Esplanade. It was one of eleven fitted with top covers in 1930, but was withdrawn and scrapped two years later. (RLS)

THE FIRST BUSES

The first motorbus service in the Rochdale area was operated by the Whitworth Vale Motor Omnibus Company, trading as 'The Pioneer'. Set up in 1906 by a group of Whitworth businessmen, the intention was to run a service between Rochdale and Bacup to fill the gap caused by the demise of the steam trams. Although a contemporary photograph depicts a bus showing Rochdale on its route boards, there is no evidence that the service ever ran through to the town centre, only going as far as the terminus of the Corporation's tram route, a couple of hundred yards over the Borough boundary.

Two buses were ordered from the long forgotten Highbury Motor Body Works in North London and a telegram was received at the end of June to say that they were ready for collection. A party of directors duly travelled to London to take delivery and, mindful of the publicity value, they invited any local residents who were interested to meet the party at Leicester and ride back to Whitworth on the buses. Some 23 people took up the offer, travelling down to Leicester on the train in eager anticipation. However, only one bus was complete and it broke down at Huntingdon, leaving the unfortunate travellers to return home by train.

A month later the second bus was ready and this time it was collected quietly without any publicity. The journey took three days stopping overnight at Leicester and Buxton, and it arrived safely in Whitworth escorted by some of the local residents on their bicycles. The following day the bus went on a trial spin to Bacup, where it was reported that hundreds of spectators gave it a hearty reception. The first bus eventually reached Disley where it underwent repairs.

The service started in August 1906, but before long the Company was having difficulty keeping the buses on the road, on more than one occasion both vehicles being reported to be 'eawt o' flunter'. By the end of October the situation had become so bad that operations were suspended and the staff were laid off.

However, hope springs eternal and in January 1907 the buses had been repaired and a third one purchased, so it was decided to have another go. The service ran more or less regularly for a short time but in March one of the buses was badly damaged when it burst into flames at Britannia

and had to be towed back home by a pair of horses. The company soldiered on bravely, but the buses were continually off the road and by the end of 1908, with Rochdale's electric trams soon to be extended through Whitworth, the directors bowed to the inevitable and the buses were sold for further use in Warrington.

A more long-lived service commenced in 1907 when Todmorden Corporation buses crossed the County boundary into Littleborough to meet Rochdale's new electric trams at the Summit Inn, this arrangement surviving until well into PTE days.

In 1921 Holt Bros (Rochdale) Ltd who were later to become much better known as Yelloway Motor Services, applied to run buses from Rochdale to Wardle and Hollingworth Lake but this was refused and two years later a local man, a Mr F Biggin, was granted a licence to run between Smallbridge and Wardle but this soon ceased.

With its compact network of tram routes, Rochdale Council saw no need for motorbuses in the Borough, but the wolves were gathering on the borders in the shape of Ribble Motor Services and the North Western Road Car Company. At that time, before the 1930 Road Traffic Act put bus service licensing into the hands of the Government's Traffic Commissioners, individual councils issued licences for bus companies to ply for hire within their area. Ribble was the first to act, in October 1923, applying to run two services, Blackburn to Rochdale via Edenfield and Norden, and Burnley to Rochdale via Todmorden and Littleborough. Both services would run over tram routes within the Borough.

Rochdale Council had no problem with either proposal, provided that there was protection for their parallel tram routes, and Ribble's maroon and cream Leylands began to appear in Rochdale town centre on the two-hourly Blackburn service in July 1924. Soon afterwards, the frequency was doubled with additional two-hourly journeys to Burnley. Despite this, the buses were often overcrowded, especially on late journeys out of Norden, on one occasion 49 passengers being recorded on a bus licenced for 32, with several said to be hanging on to the step. The service was later extended to Preston and eventually to Blackpool. Cut back by stages to Blackburn and later to Rawtenstall, the service, by then operated by Rossendale Transport, was finally withdrawn in 2005, leaving Edenfield Road beyond Norden without any bus service whatsoever.

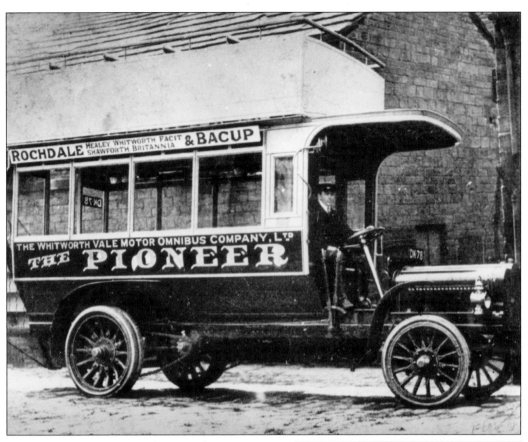

The Whitworth Vale Motor Omnibus Company could rightly call itself 'The Pioneer' as it ran the first ever bus service in the Rochdale area. However, the nearest it ever got to the town centre was to connect with the Corporation's trams at Healey. The epic journey of the first bus from London was marked by a mock memorial card circulated throughout Whitworth, much to the embarrassment of the owners. *(RLS)*

IN LOVING MEMORY OF THE
Whit'oth Motor Bus,
Which fell asleep on Saturday, June 30th, 1906.
At Huntingdon,
AGED 2 DAYS AND 4 HOURS;
And was respectfully interred by sorrowing relatives at Leicester, July 1st.

A year later Todmorden Corporation's Critchley-Norris buses crossed the County boundary to meet Rochdale's trams at the Summit Inn, Littleborough. The service still operates today as part of First West Yorkshire's 589/590 from Rochdale to Halifax and Burnley. *(RLS)*

But trouble was brewing on the other Burnley route. By September 1923 Ribble had obtained licences from Burnley Corporation and Burnley Rural District and had applied for similar facilities in Todmorden, "on such conditions as would safeguard the Corporation's own services". Since then, however, Todmorden had obtained the Ministry of Transport's consent to operate outside the Borough boundary where it was now in active competition with Ribble's own services, and had refused to issue licences to the company to ply for hire in Todmorden.

The dispute went to an appeal, held in Todmorden Town Hall on Tuesday 25th March 1924, at which Ribble were successful. Rochdale then issued a licence for the portion of the route within the Rochdale Borough and the service commenced operation in the September. Ribble operated the route for many years as its X4 service between Manchester and Burnley, even extending it to Blackpool during the summer for a few years, and it still runs today between Rochdale and Burnley as First West Yorkshire's 589.

Ribble also applied for services to Halifax and Huddersfield via Littleborough, but Rochdale turned these down. The company appealed to the Ministry of Transport who upheld Rochdale's decision.

Also in 1923 Holt Bros started running a number of bus routes in Shaw and Saddleworth. Crompton Urban District Council was none too happy with the reliability of the services and when, early in 1924, North Western proposed to operate two routes between Rochdale and Delph, one via Broad Lane, Shaw and Grains Bar, and the other via Milnrow, Newhay and Denshaw, they welcomed the competition and granted permission. This appears to have upset Oldham Corporation, which was operating trams within Crompton on the section of the proposed route between Shaw town centre and Wren's Nest and apparently had not been consulted. Eventually, agreement was reached on a revised application, with the service re-routed in Shaw to avoid the tram route.

Rochdale, meanwhile, were having tentative discussions with Halifax, Huddersfield, Oldham and Ashton-under-Lyne Corporations and the grandly named Stalybridge, Hyde, Mossley and Dukinfield Tramways and Electricity Board, with a view to operating bus services within their combined areas. The two proposed services in which Rochdale had a direct interest were to Halifax (of which more later) and to Delph along exactly the same line of route as the North Western application. Rochdale kept delaying a decision on this and from 16th October 1924 the company started running services turning at the Borough boundary at Broad Lane, and at Newhay respectively. Meanwhile, they wrote to Rochdale several times asking for the matter to be dealt with urgently.

Eventually, in June 1925 the General Manager of the Ashton-under-Lyne Corporation Tramways, Mr CI Baker, wrote to the Council on behalf of the Joint Control Committee" asking for the relevant consents within Rochdale. The Watch Committee immediately agreed and informed North Western that in view of this they could not see their way to granting its application to run within Rochdale. However, Milnrow District Council refused permission for the service between Rochdale and Delph via Denshaw. Holts withdrew their services soon afterwards to concentrate on their char-a-banc business.

The grandiose scheme never got off the ground, and in November 1926 North Western approached Rochdale with a proposal for a joint service between Rochdale and Shaw via Broad Lane and High Crompton. Agreement was reached on this and the service commenced on 17th August 1927. Rossendale Transport's service 435 still links Rochdale with Shaw by broadly the same route today.

The Denshaw route had a more varied career with North Western operating an infrequent service between Friezland and Newhay for many years before withdrawing it completely in the 1960s. Thirty years later twice-weekly journeys were re-introduced between Friezland and Rochdale, finally achieving North Western's ambitions of some 70 years earlier; long after the company itself had vanished from the scene.

THE ROCHDALE BILL

Although Rochdale Council was satisfied that its tramway network was adequate, the same could not be said of the residents of those parts of the town away from the tracks, notably Deeplish and Shawclough. For some time there had been representations and complaints from these areas and news of proposals for buses to serve Rochdale from out of town did not escape their notice. At the same time the Council woke up to the implications and, in the summer of 1924, the Tramways General Manager, Mr George Webster, produced a scheme for a small number of motor-omnibus routes linking with the tram services and filling in the more contentious gaps. Mr Webster's proposals were received enthusiastically and the Council agreed to promote a General Powers Bill in the next session of Parliament, including, amongst other matters, authority to run motor omnibuses within and outside the Borough.

When the Bill came before the House of Lords Local Legislation Committee on 18th February 1925 Rochdale were supported by Littleborough, Milnrow and Wardle District Councils and a representative of the employers in Castleton. There were seven objectors, Heywood and Middleton Boroughs, Royton and Crompton Urban District Council, The Middleton Electric Traction Company, Ribble Motor Services and the London, Midland and Scottish Railway, all on grounds of abstraction of traffic from their services, plus the Rochdale Workhouse and Poor Law Union. It is difficult to imagine why the latter would want to object to the provision of bus services, but it was probably a misunderstanding as it quickly withdrew.

At the Hearing the railway representative commented that if the powers requested were granted, there would be nothing to stop the Corporation from running buses as far as London if they wished, provided they got the permission of all the relevant local authorities. To this Mr Webster replied that they wanted to run as far as Manchester and that "*they were negotiating with other districts to provide for a great scheme of communication that would be greatly in the interests of the public*".

The House of Lords' decision was that Rochdale Council should be allowed to operate within a five-mile radius of the Town Hall and beyond that limit on any route on which they were, or might be, empowered to run tramways. This latter concession was unusual and was very valuable and important, as it granted Rochdale its wish to run buses to Manchester once the Middleton company had been wound up a few months later and the through tram service had commenced.

It also cleared the way for Rochdale's participation in the great express network that was to commence two years later. In view of Mr Webster's comments at the Hearing, it suggests that Rochdale Council, already in discussions on the cross-Pennine scheme, was also talking privately to Manchester about running a through bus service over what would by then be an existing tram route, perhaps even then as part of a much larger network of similar services, and one may wonder what groundwork the powerful Manchester political lobby had already done.

THE CORPORATION BUS

The Corporation Bill received the Royal Assent on 24th June, becoming the Rochdale Corporation Act 1925, and the Council moved quickly on three fronts. The Borough Surveyor was asked to submit a scheme for the erection of a garage for ten buses in Mellor Street adjoining the tram shed, a Sub-Committee was sent to the Commercial Motor Show at London's Olympia with power to purchase ten buses, and letters were written to Heywood, Littleborough, Milnrow, Norden, Wardle and Whitworth Urban Districts and Bury Rural District for permission to run motor omnibuses in their respective areas.

Now it had started, the Council was not going to let grass grow under its feet. After some deliberation land was purchased on the opposite side of Mellor Street from the tram shed and the proposed bus garage specification was amended to accommodate up to twenty vehicles. Plans were quickly drawn up and in January 1926 the tender for the construction of the depot was awarded to the local firm of R & T Howarth at a price of £4,200, and construction proceeded apace.

The appointment of an Omnibus Sub-Committee to travel to Olympia, rather than ordering buses straight away, raised a few eyebrows when the full Council discussed it. Alderman Taylor, the chairman of the Tramways Committee, defended the decision on the grounds that some very great improvements in bus construction would be on show there. However, the buses in which the improvements had been embodied could not be ordered until the show. Thus, if Rochdale had gone forward and ordered buses earlier, he said, the vehicles would have been out of date before the next spring, which was when it was intended to start running the services.

Interestingly, the same meeting approved the purchase of 5 new tramcars at a cost of £11,000 to work the through route to Manchester. One councillor commented on this, as in his view buses would ultimately supersede tramcars, to which Alderman Taylor replied that, in the opinion of those people most experienced in transport, this was certainly not the case. Five years later Rochdale would become one of the first major operators in the North West to start replacing its tramway network with buses, and by the end of 1932 trams would be just a memory.

The Sub-Committee duly visited the Commercial Motor Show and ordered the following:

- Guy Motors Ltd of Wolverhampton – Three chassis for 26-seater body, 30-34 hp engine,
- Dennis Brothers Ltd of Guildford – Three Dennis 16ft wheelbase passenger chassis, 60-70 hp engine,
- One Dennis 30 cwt chassis, 20 hp engine, the chassis to be fitted with the Dennis standard box van body,
- Strachan and Brown Ltd, North Acton, London – Three omnibus bodies of the 26-seater type for one-man-operation, with emergency doors at the rear,
- Strachan and Brown Ltd - Three omnibus bodies, 33-seater type with front and rear entrances.

They deferred a decision on the remaining four buses.

Meanwhile Mr Webster had drawn up detailed proposals for bus services within the Borough and the surrounding districts. These were:

- A half-hourly service via Drake Street (starting near the Wellington Hotel), Maclure Road, Milkstone Road, Deeplish Road, Well i' th' Lane and Queensway to Albion Street (Castleton), returning by the same route, requiring 2 omnibuses of the larger type,
- A one-hourly service (starting near the Lancashire and Yorkshire Bank) via Newgate, Blackwater Street, St Mary's Gate, Toad Lane, Falinge Road into Shawclough Road, connecting with the tramway at Healey Corner, requiring a one-man-operated omnibus,
- A one-hourly service between Rochdale and Wardle Village requiring an omnibus of the larger type,
- A half-hourly service between the Tramway terminus at Bamford and Jericho requiring a one-man-operated omnibus,
- A half-hourly service between Shore Road and Pyke House, Littleborough requiring a one-man-operated omnibus.

The Littleborough local route was later re-designated as two separate services from Littleborough Square to Shore and to Durn (Pyke House). Although they were to be worked by the same bus there were two separate licences and fare tables with no through booking across Littleborough. This practice was to become the norm on cross-town services in Rochdale and would last until the final demise of Corporation working. In fact, in later years, the service from Newhay to Littleborough Summit ran on three road service licences and was shown in the public timetable as three separate services, each with its own individual timetable and fares which were combined for a through journey.

The proposals called for all six buses to be in operation. It is not recorded what was intended to happen if one was to be out of service.

GETTING STARTED

The buses arrived in ones and twos during 1926, the small normal control Guys carrying the numbers 1-3 (DK3443-5) and the larger forward control Dennises 4-6 (DK3446-8). There is some confusion regarding the seating capacity of the E type Dennis, the tender specifying 33 seats although most fleet lists show it as 30. Whether the seating was changed before delivery or later is not known.

The livery was a rich shade of brown with cream round the windows, a grey roof and black rear dome down to the waistline. By the middle of March the first two Guys had arrived, so on the 17th March 1926, after posing with the Tramways Committee in front of the Town Hall, bus number 1 left Rochdale for Castleton on what would appropriately become service number 1 when route numbers were introduced five years later. The third Guy arrived soon after and was immediately put to work on the Healey route, starting on the 26th March, although Ministry of Transport sanction had not yet been received for the short section between the Borough boundary and Healey Corner.

The surrounding local authorities agreed

On 17th March 1926 the Tramways Committee and other civic dignitaries line up in front of Guy B-type single-decker number 1 for the official photograph. The bus then left on its first journey to Castleton via Deeplish. *(RLS)*

to Rochdale's proposals, although Norden intimated that they would object unless they were compensated for any damage to the road surface caused by the buses. Rochdale naturally refused and Norden pragmatically accepted defeat.

There were also two objections to the Wardle service, one from the Wardle Ratepayers, which appears to have been against Rochdale Corporation running in Wardle rather than to the service itself and the other from Mr Biggin, who had previously operated unsuccessfully on the route and would seem to have been a case of sour grapes. Wardle Council, which had supported Rochdale from the start, was actively pro-bus as it was over a mile to walk to the Halifax Road tram route, and the objections were withdrawn. With everything cleared, Lancashire County Council approved the applications and the Ministry of Transport gave consent.

Meanwhile, a petition had been received from the residents of Shawclough and Lowerfold against the service running through to Healey Corner, and asking for it to turn round at Lowerfold Chapel. The council rejected the request and the way was now open for the other routes to start.

The first two Dennises came in May and enabled the Wardle service to start on the 24th and that to Jericho three days later, the latter with one of the Guys displaced by a new Dennis from the Castleton route, which was already becoming overcrowded. These early routes were proving very popular and patronage was growing rapidly, so much so that in July the Tramways Committee approved the purchase of the four buses outstanding from the original order. These were to be Dennis E-types with Strachan and Brown bodies identical to numbers 4-6.

However, there were rumblings in the council chamber that services were being provided for non-ratepayers while there were ratepayers in the Borough who were not being served. A move to withdraw the Jericho route and run instead to Turf Hill, a new council estate on the south side of the town, was defeated, but one councillor commented that if the Tramways Committee should fall among thieves on the road to Jericho, then they should not expect a Good Samaritan to come to their aid.

Two views of Dennis E-types at Wardle terminus in 1926. In the upper photograph the crew stand proudly in front of number 4, while in the lower picture passengers wait to board a Rochdale bound bus in the village square. The colour scheme was the same dark brown as the trams, with white window surrounds, a grey roof and a black rear dome. The bus had match-boarded ceilings, cord operated bells and lamps set in glass bowls standing out from the ceiling. The seats were red leather with metal grab rails. Both the gear lever and the push-on hand brake were to the right of the driver and when the bus was parked in neutral with the hand brake on he needed to be somewhat of a contortionist to get in and out of the cab. *(RLS)*

THE FIRST ACCIDENT

The first recorded accident involving a Corporation bus occurred on 24th October 1926 when one of the Guys was heading out of Rochdale bound for Healey. Being a quiet Sunday morning the opportunity was taken to train a new driver on the route, the regular driver standing on the platform beside him.

As the trainee negotiated the sharp left up-hill turn from Cheetham Street into Red Cross Street he lost control and ran into the front of Mrs Tuck's grocery shop, finishing up embedded in the doorway, scattering stock and narrowly missing Mrs Tuck's pet dog which was in the shop at the time.

There were four passengers on the bus, two of whom were taken to hospital and treated for cuts and shock. One of the other passengers said, "The driver seemed unable to turn and we ran straight into the doorway of the shop. It was like a moving picture taken from a train when you can see the mouth of a tunnel coming nearer and nearer and then all goes black. I was sitting at the back of the bus and I was powerless to do anything. I just held on tight and braced my foot against the floor so as to meet the shock. The driver was apparently a novice for another driver in uniform was standing on the step."

The accident caused questions to be asked in Council about the training of new drivers and resulted in a tightening up of the system.

LITTLEBOROUGH

Meanwhile, there was continuing consultation with Littleborough on the proposed local service there. Littleborough Council first asked for alternate journeys on the Shore service to be diverted along Calderbrook Road to serve the new council housing at Clough Road. Rochdale were unhappy about the condition of Calderbrook Road, but Littleborough then also asked for the Durn service to be extended further up Blackstone Edge to the Moorcock Inn, and presented a petition for a service to Rakewood, a tiny hamlet round the back of Hollingworth Lake.

There was only one bus available for the foreseeable future to serve Littleborough, so a compromise was reached, which resulted in an hourly service from Hollingworth Lake to Littleborough Square via Smithy Bridge, going forward on alternate hours to Shore or Clough Road, and a promise to look again at the other proposals when a bus became available.

This suited Rochdale very well on two counts. Firstly, Hollingworth Lake, known locally as 'The Weavers' Seaport', was a popular recreational venue throughout the year and, together with the village of Smithy Bridge, would bring in much more revenue than the thinly populated slopes of Blackstone Edge beyond Durn.

Secondly, there was a rival on the scene in the shape of Mr Harry Shaw, a local haulage contractor and char-a-banc owner, who had applied to run a bus service between Littleborough and Smithy Bridge via Hollingworth Lake, and it was necessary to neutralise him.

The final Dennis arrived in August 1926 and went to work on the Castleton service, releasing a Guy to operate the one-man Littleborough local service from the 13th August. Mr Shaw saw his potential profits ebbing away and did not pursue his application, leaving Rochdale a monopoly in the Littleborough area. The Hollingworth Lake service was soon extended from the Beach Hotel to the Fisherman's Inn, further round the lake, but this was the nearest buses ever got to Rakewood.

Enthusiasm for bus services was running high and requests were made for more routes, but before these could be progressed the Council's attention was diverted elsewhere.

OVER THE EDGE

On the crest of the Pennines, the high ridge of Blackstone Edge dominates the small town of Littleborough and forms the watershed between the Irish and North Seas and more significantly the historical boundary between Lancashire and Yorkshire. In 1698 that inveterate traveller Celia Fiennes wrote that it was *"noted over all England for a dismal precipice"* and a few years later, in 1724, Daniel Defoe called it *"a frightful, narrow and precipitous place"*.

The route over Blackstone Edge has always been important in transport history. Three roads cross the Edge; the modern A58 was opened as a turnpike in 1766, rebuilt in 1824 by John Macadam and is now mainly superseded by the M62 motorway further to the south-east. Then there is the old packhorse road and the remains of a paved causeway, said to be of Roman origin. The White House inn at the summit, with its

In July 1927 Rochdale Corporation took delivery of three Dennis F-types. These differed from the E-type in being normal-control where the driver sat behind the engine and therefore suitable for one-man operated routes to Jericho and Healey and in Littleborough where the first Guys were struggling to operate the service with no spare cover. Their Strachan and Brown bodies were basically a shortened version of the F-types. *(JHC)*

long-range views across both counties was, as its former name, the Coach and Horses indicates, a stopping place for the stagecoaches running between Manchester and Leeds.

As far back as 1924 Ribble had applied to Rochdale Council for powers to run buses in the town on services to Blackburn, Burnley, Halifax and Huddersfield but, although the first two services were agreed, and indeed were proving well used, those crossing the county boundary to Halifax and Huddersfield were turned down. Ribble had appealed to the Minister of Transport, but without success.

The idea of a joint committee of municipal undertakings to run bus services throughout a large area including Rochdale and Halifax has already been mentioned. The scheme was agreed at a conference in Huddersfield on 12th September 1924, and the following year Rochdale Council authorised services to Halifax and Huddersfield. The consortium never got off the ground, but existed at least in name for some time, and the powers remained valid.

During 1926 two independents, the Ryburn Carriage and Transport Company of Sowerby Bridge, and the Ripponden and District Motor Company, both of whom had been operating in

the area for a number of years, applied to Halifax Corporation for powers to operate services from Halifax, via Sowerby Bridge, Ripponden and over Blackstone Edge Moor to Littleborough and Rochdale, but both applications were turned down.

Representatives of Halifax and Rochdale met in August 1926 and agreed to run a joint service between the two towns, although as Rochdale did not have any spare buses, Halifax were to provide all the vehicles for the time being. Halifax then applied to Littleborough District Council for powers to run the service, with Rochdale's support, and at the same time the Ryburn Company applied for a service between Sowerby Bridge and Rochdale. Littleborough Council's decision to grant Halifax powers, but to refuse Ryburn, would eventually go to appeal, but meanwhile, a week later on 26th August 1926, Halifax started running.

The service proved popular from the start and within a few weeks there were complaints of overcrowding; buses were said to be leaving Rochdale full and local passengers were unable to board in Littleborough Square. There were also complaints of speeding through Littleborough, and at Rochdale County Police Court on 2nd

March 1927 two bus drivers, William Charles Smith and Samuel Leslie Thompson, both of Halifax, were summoned for exceeding the speed limit with motorbuses. Smith's speed was stated to have been over 28 miles an hour, compared with the permitted speed of 12 miles per hour. The defendant pleaded not guilty and contended that his speed was much less than had been stated. A previous conviction in respect of a rear number plate offence was noted. Thompson, against whom nothing was known, pleaded guilty to travelling at over 16 miles per hour. Both were fined £1. The prosecution denied that the police wanted to impede or harass the bus service, but stated that there had been several complaints from the public about the speed of the buses, hence the police being sent to trap them.

Rochdale's hopes that the Halifax service would satisfy Littleborough's wish for a local route up Blackstone Edge were dashed as the Council quickly came back with it's original request for a service to the Moorcock, but now extended to the top of Blackstone Edge to serve the workers building the new waterworks there. Mr Webster, facing a stormy council meeting, promised that a local service would be introduced as soon as the new buses, currently on order, were delivered. This, however, was to be some time as the Corporation had other priorities.

In December the Ministry of Transport withheld consent for the Rochdale to Halifax service, and also for Rochdale's proposed Blackstone Edge route. Halifax sent a delegation to the Ministry and lobbied the West Riding County Council with no success, although the service was allowed to continue pending an appeal. Rochdale, with other uses for their new buses, made no attempt to implement their service.

The Ministry of Transport Enquiry into Rochdale Council's application to operate a bus service between Rochdale town centre and Blackstone Edge (White House) was held at Rochdale Town Hall on 18th March 1927. They were supported by Littleborough Urban District. Opposing the application, Ripponden and District and the Ryburn Carriage Company stated that they were not against the service to Blackstone Edge, but were objecting to the through service between Rochdale and Halifax as they had both operated along part of the route for several years.

With no opposition Rochdale's application was granted and the service commenced on 22nd June 1927. A similar Enquiry, held at Halifax on 8th April, turned down Halifax Corporation's appeal on the Rochdale route, but they kept on running until the West Riding County Council threatened to take them to the High Court. Halifax withdrew from the service on 5th February 1928, Rochdale taking it over the following day. The County Council then threatened Rochdale with similar action.

By now the Railway Road Transport Act had been passed, allowing the railways to operate

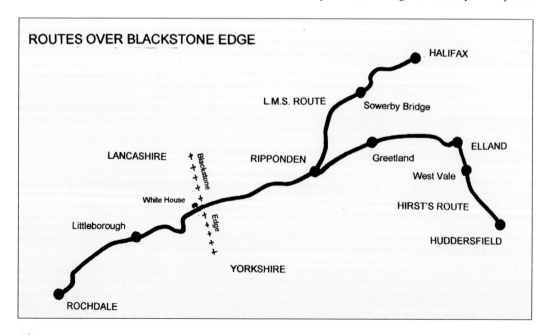

ROUTES OVER BLACKSTONE EDGE

bus services, either directly or through subsidiary companies. This offered a way out of the impasse and representatives of Rochdale and Halifax Corporations and the London Midland and Scottish Railway Company met in Halifax on 27th July to resolve the position. Agreement was reached whereby the LMS would run the service between Halifax and Rochdale town centres, extended to the railway stations at either end, on the basis that the costs and receipts were divided equally between all three parties. The agreement also included the Corporation's Rochdale to Blackstone Edge service and the railway shared in the operation of these journeys.

The LMS took over the operation on 3rd December 1928 using Leyland Lions bodied in their own workshops at Derby. Later they transferred it to Hebble Motor Services of Halifax, a company by then acquired by the railway. Hebble started running on 10th December 1933, abandoning the extensions to the railway stations, increasing the frequency and reducing the fares. The service eventually passed to the Halifax Joint Omnibus Committee and survives today as the Huddersfield Bus Company's 528.

However, there were other ramifications. As a matter of policy, the railway companies had objected to any applications by councils to run outside the area covered by their Parliamentary powers, and part of the agreement was that both Halifax and Rochdale "acknowledged the railways' interest" in such services, and that if this was agreed, then the LMS. would not object to any more such applications. In the case of Halifax this would eventually result in the formation of the Halifax Joint Committee, and in Rochdale five existing services, Rochdale to Bury via Jericho, Bacup to Manchester, Rochdale to Todmorden, Rochdale to Oldham and Ashton, and Rochdale to Shaw became nominally joint with the LMS No attempt was made to influence the operation of these routes except for the Rochdale to Bury service, which was extended to Rochdale railway station for a short time.

But this was not quite the end of the story. Early in 1930 John Hirst and Company of Commercial Garage, Ripponden, applied to Rochdale and Littleborough Corporations for a licence to operate a bus service between Huddersfield and Rochdale via Elland, West Vale, Greetland, Barkisland, Ripponden and Littleborough. Hirst was the owner of the Ripponden and District Company and this was an extension of the service he already ran between Elland and Ripponden. Both Rochdale and Littleborough refused the application, Hirst appealed and it went to an Enquiry at Rochdale Town Hall on 5th March 1930.

Rochdale and Littleborough both argued that the LMS service between Halifax and Rochdale was adequate for the traffic over that section of the route. Hirst, on the other hand, contended that passengers wanting to travel between Ripponden and Rochdale often had to wait anything up to three hours before they could board a bus and produced, as witness, a Mr William Gledhill, a paper bag manufacturer from Greetland, who claimed he needed to travel to Rochdale three or four times a week in the course of his business and often had to stay the night in Rochdale as he could not get a bus home. Mr Percy Gray, the Ministry of Transport Inspector conducting the enquiry, was singularly unimpressed and rejected the appeal.

Hirst did try once more later in the year, applying for a service between Huddersfield and Rochdale via Outlane, Denshaw and Newhay. This was opposed by Rochdale, Halifax and Huddersfield Corporations and was refused by the newly created Traffic Commissioners. Hirst then gave up trying and eventually withdrew from bus operation to concentrate on the haulage side of the business.

A TIME OF GROWTH

The four outstanding buses from the original ten arrived towards the end of 1926. These were more Dennis E-types with 30-seat bodies by Strachan and Brown, identical to the last three delivered. Numbered 7-10 (DK3841-4), they were intended for the Blackstone Edge and Turf Hill routes. As the former was, at that time, the subject of a Ministry of Transport Enquiry, the Turf Hill service came first, commencing on 22nd October. It followed the Castleton service as far as the railway station, then ran along Milkstone Road, Well I' th' Lane, Platting Lane and Broad Lane, before taking a circular route through the estate, thus avoiding the Oldham Road tram route. The estate roads were narrow, and in March 1927 the service was routed both ways along Turf Hill Road to terminate at Neston Road. Following complaints from residents who had lost their service, the terminus was later moved further

One of the earlier Strachan and Brown-bodied Dennis E-types stands outside the Electric House in Smith Street, while the rear end of a North Western Road Car bus on the Shaw service appears on the right of the picture. *(RLS)*

along Turf Hill Road to Ansdell Road. The other buses were kept in reserve as the strain of running six all-day workings with six buses was beginning to tell.

The popularity of the first bus services had far exceeded expectations, and requests came in for more routes. Consequently, in February 1927 the council agreed to the General Manager's plans to expand the network, purchase ten more buses, and extend the Mellor Street garage to accommodate them. The opportunity was also taken to set up a dedicated motorbus section within the Tramways Department, headed by Mr Robert Farrar who, as the bus operation grew, was to become Traffic Manager and eventually Deputy General Manager. The contract for the depot extension again went to Messrs R and T Howarth for the sum of £3,000.

In March, following representations from residents, the Jericho service was diverted off Bury Road along War Office Lane and Norden Road to serve Bamford Village. However, the

poor state of War Office Lane caused severe damage to the little Guys which worked it and so, with the exception of a couple of peak hour workmen's journeys, the service quickly reverted to the main road. The residents were not amused, and demanded that Bury Rural District, in whose area Bamford lay at that time, should repair the road surface. It took some time to raise the money and carry out the work, and by then Rochdale had a different solution to the problem.

Initially, only seven of the ten buses authorised were ordered. These were more Strachan and Brown-bodied Dennises, four 30-seat E-types and three 26-seat normal control F-types. Delivery commenced in the July and they were numbered 11-17 (DK4190-6). The first three enabled two new services to be started on 26th July 1927; to Syke via Newgate, Blackwater Street, Spotland Road, Hudson Street, Heights Lane, Quarry Street, Whitehall Street, Mizzy Road, Fieldhouse Road and Dewhirst Road, and the other a circular

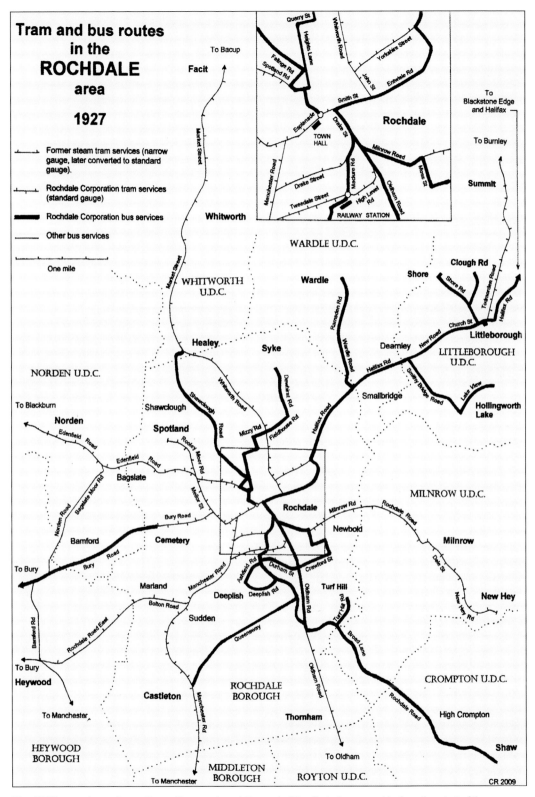

The 1927 map shows the pattern of bus routes at the end of the first phase, and before the start of the express network. The tramway system is also at its maximum extent before the first conversions took place. *(CR)*

route via Milnrow Road, Moss Street, St Peter's Street, Vavasour Street, Crawford Street, across Oldham Road into Durham Street and Milkstone Road to the railway station then back to the town centre via Maclure Road and Drake Street.

Three weeks later, on 17th August 1927, North Western's service from Piethorn via Newhay and Shaw to the Rochdale boundary at High Crompton was extended through to Rochdale via Broad Lane and Oldham Road, with the Corporation and the company providing one bus each.

The two local routes served to show up the divisions within the Council. In the September there was heated discussion on the Syke service, revolving around the state of the roads in Syke, and whose responsibility it was to pay for the work needed to upgrade them for use by buses. Accusations and counter-accusations were thrown backwards and forwards about the advisability of starting the bus service before the roads were made suitable, but it was essentially a chicken and egg situation as, without the bus service the roads would not have been improved for many years.

Then a problem arose with the Circular. This service was not doing well, and the Tramways Committee wanted to extend the route around the Deeplish area to pull in some more revenue and help out the hard-pressed Castleton service.

The Watch Committee, which at that time was responsible for issuing licences, refused to do so on the grounds that the proposed route was unsuitable. A similar situation had arisen in neighbouring Oldham some time earlier, and a dispute had followed between the respective committees before the Town Clerk had ruled that the Watch Committee had no jurisdiction to over-rule the Tramways Committee on such matters.

However, the Rochdale Tramways Committee did not press the point and a Sub-Committee was set up to look at alternatives. After due deliberation they recommended withdrawing the service and it came off on Christmas Eve 1927. Five days earlier, on 19th December, alternate buses on the Cemetery to Jericho service, which linked the tramway services of Rochdale and Bury and was far from convenient for passengers making the through journey, had been extended at either end to run between Rochdale and Bury every 30 minutes.

Other services were planned to start during 1928. One was a circular route to serve Bamford Village, travelling along Mellor Street, Edenfield Road, Bagslate Moor Road, Norden Road, War Office Lane and Bury Road, requiring one bus in each direction on a 40-minute frequency. However, the problem of War Office Lane had not yet been resolved and it was not to be implemented until the following March. The other service was a short route to the Printers' Arms at Belfield via Entwisle Road, Hamer Lane and Belfield Road, which was achieved at no cost by extending the Healey service. This started on 9th December 1928. With local demand largely satisfied for the time being, the Tramways Committee turned their minds to greater things.

THE EXPRESS SERVICES

As far back as the House of Lords Select Committee considering the Rochdale Corporation Bill, Mr Edwards, the General Manager, had made no secret of his wish to operate bus services through to Manchester, nor indeed to other destinations, over and above existing tram routes. But that was 1925 and at that time Rochdale did not yet have any buses, nor were there any plans to use them outside the immediate area when they did come. Further, the Council had already dealt with what competition had arisen, either refusing licences or coming to an accommodation, as with North Western and Ribble.

Neighbouring Manchester was perceived as a revenue gold mine, and Ribble, North Western and a host of small independents were actively trying to get their hands on it. Henry Mattinson, Manchester's forward-thinking General Manager, decided to take the battle to the enemy. Until then Manchester, like most other municipal operators, had viewed buses solely as feeders to its trams, but Mr Mattinson proposed a network of cross-city express services, running beyond the city boundaries, into the surrounding districts where Manchester had operating rights, stopping only at tramway fare stages and charging minimum fares double that of the trams.

The first service started on 11th April 1927 between Heywood and Cheadle, but before further routes could be implemented, the other municipal operators in the area expressed an interest in taking part. So, in August 1927, a conference was held at Oldham attended by representatives from Ashton-

Driver and conductor pose in front of new Dennis E-type number 20, the first of a batch of eleven buses delivered in 1928 for the Manchester express services. These differed from previous vehicles of the type in having a sloping windscreen and curved top to the cab door window, compared to number 4 on page 15. They were also fitted with Eco roller blind destination boxes. *(RLS)*

under-Lyne, Bolton, Bury, Manchester, Oldham, Rochdale, Salford and Stockport Corporations and the SHMD Joint Board, at which agreement was reached in principle to create a co-ordinated network of jointly-operated through services between Manchester and the various towns around, following which a revised list of services was prepared.

In October the Tramways Committee approved the purchase of a further eight buses, three of which had previously been authorised by the council. Again these were to be Strachan and Brown-bodied Dennises of both E- and F-types, which would come in two batches and be numbered 18-20 (DK4197-9) and 21-5 (DK4682-6). From number 20 onward the windscreen was sloping instead of vertical as in the previous E-types and seating was increased to 32. The buses were fitted with a roller blind destination box at the front, the existing vehicles being retrofitted in due course.

Rochdale's first involvement in the express service network was the Manchester route, alternately to Cannon Street and Cornbrook, which followed the tramway through Castleton and Middleton, commencing on 24th October 1927. To keep short riders off the service, a minimum fare twice that on the trams was charged. The value of the clause in the Rochdale Corporation Act allowing the Corporation to run buses over existing tram services was clearly apparent as the proposals went through without any objections.

Although the story of the Manchester-centred network is better known, Rochdale had other interests of its own. In March 1927 Hebble Motor Services of Halifax had applied to Rochdale and Todmorden Corporations for powers to run a bus service between Halifax and Rochdale via Hebden Bridge, Todmorden and Littleborough. Their application was turned down, and Hebble do not appear to have taken it any further. However, it seems to have given both Councils food for thought as, after unofficial discussions, representatives of Rochdale and Todmorden met formally on 2nd December to agree the details of a 40-minute interval express service, worked by one bus from each operator. The service started on 26th January 1928, the LMS Railway put in an objection and the matter went to appeal, although the service continued.

At the Ministry of Transport Enquiry at Rochdale Town Hall on 20th March 1928, the Town Clerk of Rochdale laid great emphasis on the provisions of the Rochdale Corporation Act, pointing out that they already ran trams from Rochdale to Littleborough Summit, where they met the Todmorden Corporation buses. He contended that both Corporations had the right to enter into a through running agreement without needing the authority of the Ministry of Transport, provided that the service was operated over existing routes for which powers had already been granted. This argument was accepted by the railway company, which then based its appeal on the standard grounds of abstraction of passengers and loss of revenue.

Summing up, Major Tolerton, for the Ministry of Transport, confirmed Rochdale's interpretation of the Act and added that while it was clear that the bus service would affect the railway, nobody could say to what extent. In due course the appeal was rejected.

In November 1927 while discussions on further proposals were taking place, Holt Brothers (Rochdale) Limited, who had previously operated a short-lived service between Bamford and Heywood and a network of services around Shaw and Saddleworth, and were by now trading as Yelloway Motor Services, jumped in and started a 20-minute service from Rochdale to Manchester via Royton and Chadderton, run on an express licence. The service lasted until 1944, when Yelloway sold it to Rochdale, Oldham and Manchester Corporations.

For some time talks had also been going on with Bacup and Whitworth councils on an express service from Rochdale to Bacup, again following the existing tram route. As the discussions continued they developed into a proposal for a through service to Manchester incorporating the Cornbrook journeys on the recently introduced Rochdale to Manchester route. Things were moving quickly, however, and the Manchester service was extended through Stretford to Urmston on 13th February 1928 so that, by the time the Bacup service was introduced on 5th March, it ran all the way to Urmston. Ribble objected to the proposal and the Ministry of Transport Enquiry

was held on 20th March, immediately following that into the Todmorden service.

Rochdale went straight into the attack. The Town Clerk again pointed out that, as allowed by the Rochdale Corporation Act, the route was over existing tramway services and the consent of the local authorities and Lancashire County Council had been obtained. Ribble were not ratepayers of Rochdale, Whitworth or Bacup, nor did they operate a service between Bacup and Rochdale; and therefore they had no legal right to object. Accepting this, the company stated that they were not opposed to the application as it stood, but were concerned that Rochdale Corporation might want to run beyond Bacup to Burnley sometime in the future and sought assurances that they would not do so. Again the appeal was rejected. The Council was quickly setting precedents. On 24th May 1928 the service was extended further to Flixton.

At that time there was still one proposal outstanding. The Managers of Rochdale, Oldham and Ashton-under-Lyne Corporations had met on 17th January and agreed proposals for a joint half-hourly express service between Rochdale and Ashton via Royton and Oldham, again over existing tram or trolley-bus routes. Oldham would provide two buses, and Rochdale and Ashton one each, proportionate to the mileage in each area. The service started on 21st February 1928, and provided through services between the three towns that had not existed for a number of years.

Authority was given for the Mellor Street garage to be extended again, and a further five buses were ordered. These were more Dennis E-types with Strachan and Brown 32-seat bodies that would be numbered 26-30 (DK5101-5), for operating spares and for unspecified service enhancements. They were quickly followed by another order for five more Dennisses known as the ES-type carrying an improved version of the Strachan and Brown body with 31 seats. These were intended for the express services and to replace the Guys, which were now too small for the routes for which they had been bought and were not strong enough for the poor roads where they were being used. A contemporary account describes the new buses as being *"the last word in comfort and convenience"* and *"representing the acme of comfortable travel"*. It is interesting to note in the current climate, that one of their selling points was an increase in the number of seats for smokers! Other improvements were the provision of parcel racks, overhanging glass screens over the top of the windows so that they could be opened without admitting a direct draught onto the passengers and the provision of destination indicators at the rear as well as the front of the bus. They became 31-5 (DK5473-7).

When the first of the new buses was delivered the Tramways Committee and Chief Officers rode on it to the Borough boundary at Castleton and back where, over afternoon tea in the Town Hall, a self-congratulatory Alderman Clark told those present that Rochdale appeared to be one of the very few Corporations who had hit on the right type of bus when they had first undertaken this type of transport three years before. They were new to the business then, but they had gone very carefully into the question before deciding on the type of bus to adopt and they had chosen on the right lines. They had also made a wise decision in adopting a standard vehicle and sticking to it. Some people had thought that they should have tried several types, but the experience of Corporations that had done so was that they had had to keep a much larger stock of spares and their capital expenditure was also larger

Manchester's first express service, between Cheadle and Heywood, had started as far back as April 1927, the extra mile to Gatley being added the following December. Heywood Council had been complaining for some time that the town was becoming the poor relation in regard to bus services, and in August 1928 Rochdale held discussions with Manchester with a view to extending the route from Heywood to Norden via Hooley Bridge and Bamford village. The service started on 29th September 1928.

The original route ran along Bamford Road, Rochdale and Bury Old Road, Norden Road, Bagslate Moor Road and Edenfield Road, but when the improvements to War Office Lane were completed, and it was renamed War Office Road to celebrate its enhanced status, the buses started using it from 8th February 1929. Although Manchester operated the service Rochdale retained a road service licence to the end and it was nominally a joint service, with Rochdale fares being charged between Norden and Heywood Hall Gates.

A Bamford local circular service had been planned for some time, running every forty minutes in both directions via the Esplanade, Bridge Street, Bury Road, Bamford Village, and Bagslate Moor Road and returning via Edenfield Road and Mellor Street., but it had been deferred until the improvements to War Office Lane had been carried out. Now, with the new road available, it was introduced shortly afterwards on 24th March 1929, running across the town centre to the railway station and replacing the similar operation by the Bury via Jericho service which had been part of the agreement with the LMS. The routing through Bamford Village of the peak period journeys on the Jericho service was withdrawn at the same time.

Rochdale's second input into the Manchester express network came on 13th May 1929 when the Knott Mill journeys on the Manchester service were extended through to Littleborough, then three days later they were extended again, this time at the Manchester end to Altrincham.

On 12th August 1929 alternate journeys between Rochdale and Bury via Jericho had been replaced by an express service between Rochdale and Bolton, a move that was not popular with passengers using those stops between Rochdale and Bury who had lost half their service. However, in the July, discussions had been held between representatives of Rochdale, Bury and Bolton, with a view to running an express service between Bolton and Rochdale via Bury, Heap Bridge, Heywood, Marland and Sudden, to be operated jointly by the three undertakings, with Heywood paying part of the costs and taking a proportion of the revenue. The service started on 21st October 1929, and on the same day the Jericho bus reverted to its half hourly frequency between Rochdale and Bury.

Rochdale's express network was now at its maximum extent and the bus fleet had reached 32, all Dennis E- or F-types with Strachan and Brown bodies. Just one more was to come. Strachan and Brown, by now renamed Strachan (Acton) Ltd, asked if they could display one of their latest buses in Rochdale's colour scheme on their stand at the Commercial Motor Show at Olympia later in the year. The Committee accepted the invitation and agreed to purchase the bus, a Dennis EV, which became 36 (DK6028).

Now, however, another question was beginning to exercise the minds of the Council. The tramway system was becoming in need of urgent repair and, with an eye to the future and despite Alderman Clark's former forthright views to the contrary, it departed from its policy of a standard fleet and ordered an all-Crossley double-decker for evaluation. Number 37 (DK6552) would have a profound effect on the bus fleet over the next few years.

Only six months separate these two buses, yet they represent a great step forward in bus design and operating policy. Number 36 (above) was exhibited at the 1929 Commercial Motor Show and typifies the ultimate development of the combination of Dennis chassis and Strachan and Brown body. *(JHC)*
Number 37, which entered service in May 1930, was Rochdale's first double-decker. A Crossley Condor with a Crossley low-height body seating 48, with a sunken gangway either side of the upper deck, it was purchased for evaluation against the Dennis examples. Within the next two years it would be followed by a further 62 similar vehicles in both lowbridge and highbridge versions as the tramway network was swept away. *(PDC)*

TRAMS v BUSES

After the takeover of the Middleton system in 1925, the track between Sudden and the Borough boundary at Chesham Avenue, Castleton had been re-laid to double track at considerable expense, but the rest of the system was not up to the same standard, much of it being single track with passing loops. Complaints about the poor condition of the track and the rough riding of the trams were becoming more frequent. One councillor remarked that he would rather cross the English Channel on a stormy day, than ride to Bury on the top of a tram, while a Whitworth councillor, commenting on the number of breakdowns on the Bacup route, expressed the view that *"The cars would be all right if they did the axles up properly instead of tying them together with string"*.

Of particular concern, however, was the section between Littleborough town centre and Summit. As far back as 1924, when Rochdale's lease of the lines in Littleborough was due to run out, discussions had taken place at which Littleborough Council had agreed to extend the lease on the existing terms and Rochdale, for their part, had agreed to continue operating a service, although not necessarily with trams. In November 1925 the Tramways Committee had recommended reconstruction of the track, but since then their experience with bus operation had caused them to defer implementation while they considered their options. However, Littleborough Council kept pressing for a decision.

During 1928, lengthy and sometimes acrimonious discussions took place in the Council on the subject of the tram services. Two factions were rapidly developing; those who wanted to retain the trams, and an increasing number who wanted to embrace the modern image of the motorbus. Manchester Corporation's General Manager, R Stuart Pilcher, later summed up the position in a paper to the Rochdale Reform Club, in which he said that many of the arguments were psychological. The vast majority of people would sooner ride on a bus than a tram, because this was a motoring age, and the bus was the next best thing to a car. However, the only argument which carried any weight was the heavy cost of tramway reconstruction, because in times of change and uncertainty in the transport industry no local authority would be willing to commit itself to huge expenditure for twenty years ahead, and even if the track was comparatively new and not in need of immediate renewal, it might be better to abandon it and run buses which would be cheaper.

In the end this argument was incontrovertible. Costs of £17,500 for the section from the Borough boundary to Smithy Bridge Road, and £30,000 from there to Littleborough in addition to the £12,500 previously quoted for the Summit section, added up to a total of some £60,000, a huge amount in those days, the equivalent of £3,000,000 at today's prices.

In February 1929 the Council endorsed the Tramways Committee's recommendation to abandon the track from the Borough boundary at Smallbridge to Littleborough Summit and to replace it with a service of buses. This was not quite as simple as it might sound on three counts. Firstly, detailed negotiations needed to be held with Littleborough and Wardle District Councils who owned the track on which Rochdale ran the service, and they had to be satisfied about the financial implications. Secondly, buses had to be ordered to run the service and last, but by no means least, application had to be made to Parliament for powers to cease running the trams. So, in June, the Corporation resolved to promote a Bill in the next session of Parliament to enable them to abandon all or part of their tramway network, if and when it became necessary. The powers that the Corporation requested were

- to enable Rochdale to abandon its tramways and provide other services in lieu,
- to enter into agreements with any local authorities owning tramways leased to, worked by or run over by Rochdale, and
- to restrict the running of buses on any route within the Borough in competition with Rochdale's own services.

This latter clause was the only contentious one, as many applicants had tried to get similar protection but very few had succeeded.

At this time there was no intention to abandon the whole network, as the Tramways Committee's policy was to look at each line on an individual basis. It was estimated that total abandonment would require at least 53 double-deck and 27 single-deck buses at a cost in the region of £170,000, and this was not a realistic proposition. However, some economies could be made quickly, and from 4th August 1929, Sunday morning tram services were withdrawn and replaced by buses running on tram times and charging tram fares.

27

Number 49 was one of the first batch of Crossley Alphas, the single-deck version of the Condor, delivered in October 1930. Its original petrol engine was replaced by a six-cylinder Crossley oil engine in 1934. The bus remained in the brown livery until its withdrawal in 1940 when it went to the Ministry of Transport. *(PDC both)*

The Rochdale Corporation (No 2) Bill had its first reading before a Select Committee of the House of Commons on 5th and 6th May 1930, the only objector being the Lancashire County Council. Rochdale's case was that several of the existing tramways were coming to the end of their economic life. For example, the lease of the Littleborough tramways had run out some years earlier, and had been extended by agreement from time to time. The question was, what was to happen to these tramways, particularly the unpaid portion of the debt upon them, for which Littleborough was still responsible? In Rochdale's view there

could be no justification for reconstructing the tramway at a prohibitive cost, when buses could do the job as well, if not better. Rochdale had agreed to take over Littleborough's outstanding debt, but could not in all fairness be expected to do so without some protection against indiscriminate competition.

Apart from the economic argument, the public preferred the fast and comfortable bus to the slow and cumbersome tramcar, especially in a district like Rochdale where narrow roads dictated single lines with passing loops that slowed the service down. Under the Bill the Corporation would also assume an obligation for providing workmen's services at workmen's fares on any route where trams were replaced by buses, and they could not afford to do this if traffic was lost to competitors.

Lancashire County Council objected solely on the protection clause. In its view Rochdale already had sufficient protection, and had made agreements with companies and other local authorities for co-ordinated services, and they did not see the need for anything more. The previous July the County Council had convened a conference of all the local authorities in Lancashire, as a result of which a committee had been appointed to consider the traffic problems in the county and the Lancashire Traffic Board Bill had been drawn up. This Bill proposed that there should be a single traffic board covering the geographical county of Lancashire, which would take over licensing powers from the individual local authorities.

This had been agreed in principle by all the 140 local authorities in the county, including Rochdale. After the Bill had been deposited, the report of the Royal Commission on Road Traffic had been published and the Government had introduced its own Road Traffic Bill, which was currently going through Parliament. Since this Bill was similar to Lancashire's in most regards, Lancashire had withdrawn its own Bill, which would otherwise have gone forward with the agreement of Rochdale and the 139 other local authorities.

However, apart from the merits of the particular case, the County Council opposed the Bill on general principles. It contended that traffic problems over large areas could not be solved by piecemeal action, but could only be dealt with adequately by taking at least a geographical county as a unit, and that if a particular area like Rochdale were to be singled out for privileged treatment, it would prejudice the broader consideration of the question.

In view of the Road Traffic Bill currently going through Parliament, two days of arguments for and against Rochdale's Bill were, to a great extent, empty rhetoric. The Select Committee evidently thought likewise as, after only a few minutes deliberation, they found in favour of Rochdale and declined to delete the offending clause. Lancashire County Council withdrew their opposition and on 1st July the House of Lords Unopposed Bills Committee passed it. It received the Royal Assent on 10th July, passing onto the statute book as the Rochdale Corporation (General Provisions) Act 1930.

In the end Rochdale gained something of a hollow victory, as soon afterwards the Government's Bill became the Road Traffic Act 1930, taking all road service licensing away from the local authorities and transferring it to Government appointed Area Traffic Commissioners.

BUSES TO LITTLEBOROUGH

Now that the Corporation had got what it wanted, a start could be made on converting the Littleborough route. Initially, it had been planned to abandon the tramway from the Rochdale boundary at Smallbridge, through to Littleborough Summit, and to retain a tram service between Rochdale and Smallbridge, at least for the time being. To this end a provisional order had been placed in May 1930 for five Crossley double-deck buses similar to number 37. However, the state of the track within Rochdale was little better, so it was decided to convert the whole route at one go and the order was increased to fourteen, comprising eight Crossley Condor double-deckers and six Crossley Alpha single-deckers.

As there was insufficient room in the motorbus garage, it was decided to rebuild three bays on the eastern side of the tram shed to accommodate them. The pits were covered over, water supply points were provided, and a 10,000-gallon petrol tank was installed. In all, 16 of the oldest trams would be withdrawn.

Considering the top end of Yorkshire Street to be adequately covered, it was proposed to run the whole service along Entwisle Road and withdraw the journeys operating via John Street. However, the residents of Wardleworth were unhappy about this and requests were made for a circular service to run via John Street and Yorkshire Street to Heybrook, returning via Entwisle Road. Faced with this, the committee decided to revert to the long standing tramway practice of running alternate journeys via Entwisle Road or John Street, a pattern which lasted well into PTE days.

There was also concern about turning arrangements at Summit. The trams, of course, had not needed anywhere to turn, but the road was narrow and there was no suitable place for a bus terminus. In fact, for some time Todmorden buses had been turning at the county boundary at Steanor Bottom, a little further along the road towards Todmorden. Rochdale proposed either turning short or abandoning the Littleborough to Summit section entirely, but Littleborough Council eventually purchased some land at the side of the Summit Inn for both Rochdale and Todmorden buses to reverse, and enable the connection to be reinstated.

The order for Crossley buses was contentious and was the subject of lengthy debate in Council. The four-cylinder Dennis single-decker with a two-door Strachan and Brown body was the standard vehicle in the fleet, and by all accounts was reliable and cheap to run. In fact, Rochdale's running costs were, at 7.831d per mile, said to be the lowest in the country with only two exceptions, so why change to an untried six-cylinder machine from another manufacturer on the basis of some three months experience with a single example. According to Alderman Clark, the chairman of the newly renamed Passenger Transport Committee, the buses ordered were of a more modern design, the six-cylinder engine was found to be smoother and more economical in operation especially on hilly routes, and in view of the need to convert the tram service as soon as possible one great advantage was that Crossley's delivery time was shorter.

While the Manchester firm of Crossley Motors was a relative newcomer to the bus scene, having only started building complete buses in 1928, they had had considerable experience of making engines for buses and heavy commercial vehicles since 1905. Their first complete model was the Crossley Eagle single-decker with a four-cylinder petrol engine. Very few were built before the company replaced it with a six-cylinder model originally known simply as the Crossley Six, which quickly became the single-deck Alpha and double-deck Condor, the types ordered by Rochdale. The bodies were also by Crossley, the ones on the single-deckers having 32 seats similar to those on the Dennises, and the double-deckers carrying a 50-seat, six-bay piano-front lowbridge body, due to the number of low railway bridges which existed at the time. The double-deck bodies were similar to those of the same make currently in service with Manchester Corporation, having

a sunken gangway either side of the upper deck with rows of triple seats between and a metal sun visor above the driver's front windscreen.

The buses arrived in October, the eight double-deckers numbered 38-45 (DK6865-72) and the single-deckers 46-51 (DK6873-78). The last day of tram operation on the Littleborough route was Saturday 18th October 1930, buses taking over on the following day. The changeover was said to have gone very smoothly with the new service operating entirely satisfactorily.

WEST ROCHDALE

Next came the Norden route. In August 1930 the Council had decided to widen Edenfield Road beyond Churchill Street. This would have involved considerable expenditure on the tram track and overhead so the Passenger Transport Committee proposed to abandon the section between Churchill Street and Norden, and substitute a bus service between Rochdale and Norden via Mellor Street, with trams retained for peak period short workings to Churchill Street via Spotland Road. There would also be a peak period bus service between Rochdale and Spotland, also via Spotland Road. It was decided to abandon the Bury Road service at the same time.

Six more buses were ordered, three Condors, 52-4 (DK6957-9) and three Alphas, 55-7 (DK6960-2).

This complicated arrangement was devised to keep the number of buses to the minimum, but not surprisingly it provoked an outcry from the residents and shopkeepers of Spotland Road and St Mary's Gate who stood to lose their through service to Norden. It should be noted that while St Mary's Gate nowadays is part of the dual carriageway inner ring road, at that time it was a very busy shopping area. Then, the Borough Surveyor dropped the bombshell that, despite spending over £2,000 on emergency repairs to the tracks in Spotland Road, Edenfield Road and Rooley Moor Road, they were still in a dangerous state and he could no longer accept responsibility for them.

Once again the Passenger Transport Committee were forced into an embarrassing U-turn and a modified scheme was drawn up to abandon the whole of the Norden, Spotland and Bury Road routes and substitute similar bus services.

In the spring of 1931 a Crossley double-decker passes through a largely deserted Norden village, shortly after buses had replaced the trams along Edenfield Road. Although the overhead wiring has been taken down the tram track still remains. The imposing Methodist church has gone, but otherwise little has changed in the ensuing eight decades other than the modernisation of shop fronts, the covering of the stone setts and a huge rise in traffic and parked cars. *(RLS)*

A request had been made to extend some of the journeys on the Spotland route to Lanehead, a small hamlet further up Rooley Moor Road. The road surface was in poor condition, but it was agreed to go as far as Brookside, at its junction with Caldershaw Lane, to serve the mills and the new Brotherod council estate being built there, and to consider going on to Lanehead when the road was suitable.

As there were not enough buses available to carry out the full scheme, the conversion of the Spotland route was deferred. The last trams ran to Bury Road and Norden on 3rd January 1931, the replacement bus services commencing the following day with the Bamford Circular service diverted via Sandy Lane, and a supplementary service between the Cemetery and town being provided by the extension of the Castleton route.

SERVICE NUMBERING

Trams had never displayed service numbers, this being considered unnecessary with a simple radial network such as that in Rochdale. Nor was there any need for them on the few original bus services. However, numbers had been introduced in Manchester some time earlier and Rochdale's joint service to Manchester was numbered 17, although this was not displayed on Rochdale's buses.

At the meeting of the Passenger Transport Committee on 18th February 1931, it was agreed that *"a system of numbering of the omnibus routes be introduced, and that illuminated indicator signs displaying the routes and destinations be fitted to the omnibuses"*. Service numbers were included in the next edition of the timetable, but only gradually appeared on the buses.

The proposed scheme was as follows:
1 Cemetery-Rochdale-Castleton
2 Healey-Rochdale-Belfield
3 Rochdale-Littleborough

4 Rochdale-Wardle
5 Rochdale-Bamford Circular
6 Rochdale-Littleborough Summit
7 Rochdale-Oldham-Ashton
8 Littleborough local service
9 Norden-Rochdale-Thornham
10 Syke-Rochdale-Turf Hill
11 Rochdale-Blackstone Edge
12 Railway Station-Rochdale-Spotland
15 Rochdale-Shaw
16 Rochdale-Bacup
17 Rochdale-Manchester
18 Rochdale-Newhay
19 Rochdale-Bury via Jericho
20 Rochdale-Todmorden
21 Rochdale-Bury via Heywood
23 Rochdale-Bury-Bolton

The numbers took into account future tram conversions. The Blackstone Edge service was withdrawn before the scheme commenced.

When service numbers were introduced, buses that had originally had roller blinds lost them and instead were fitted with individual metal plates with black lettering on a white background. These plates slotted into brackets above the driver's cab on double-deckers and below the canopy over the bonnet of the single-deckers, with a further plate in one of the nearside saloon windows. Service numbers were displayed at the extreme near side of the front upper deck windows on double-deckers and at the front of the roof on single-deckers. Sufficient number and destination plates were carried to cover a vehicle's duty for the day.

Suffix letters to denote route variations were not included on the plates and instead boards with the letters painted on were displayed on the nearside bulkhead window. As these were not lit there was confusion especially after dark. Later plates did carry some route suffixes but this did not necessarily improve matters, as one irate passenger wrote to the local paper.

"I should like to draw the attention of the Passenger Transport Department to a great inconvenience suffered by passengers travelling to and from Sudden. The sign at Sudden informs people that the 17 and 17D buses travel via Drake Street, 23 buses via Manchester Road and 23T buses via Tweedale Street. This anyone can understand, but which way does a 17A bus travel? Some 17A buses also carry the letters 'T' or 'D', from which one understands that the bus
will travel via Tweedale Street or Drake Street accordingly. Others do not, and if you wish to go any particular way it is a case of calling for the conductor and enquiring before boarding the bus, thus causing delay. Also there are Marland and Castleton specials, which carry no indication letters.

Another thing often happens, of which I give you an instance. Wishing to travel via Manchester Road today I boarded a Bolton No 23 bus at Sudden, which I naturally thought would go via Manchester Road. However, on booking, I was informed that the bus was going along Tweedale Street. I asked the conductor why a bus No. 23 which should travel via Manchester Road, was going via Tweedale Street, and was told that the bus carried an indication letter 'T'. I then suggested that in such a case the conductor should inform people when boarding, but was told that it was not his business to do this, and that the mistake was the fault of the Corporation for not supplying the letters."

The whole subject of suffix letters is something of a tangled web and throughout the Corporation's existence they have meant different things at different times, often changing without notice.

MORE CONVERSIONS

The next tramway abandonment was intended to be the service along Oldham Road to Thornham. In view of the previous dispute about buying Crossley buses, the Transport Committee went out to tender for the next twelve, and subsequently ordered another six Alphas and six Condors. The Alphas were numbered 58-63 (DK7138-43) and the Condors 64-9 (DK7144-9). 67 was fitted with a diesel engine instead of the previously standard petrol version. Two more bays in the tram shed were converted to accommodate the buses. However, the delayed Spotland conversion needed some of these vehicles, so the Committee was again forced into a partial changeover with buses running the through service between Rochdale and Thornham while trams continued to operate the short workings to Broad Lane. Both the Thornham and the Spotland to Station services went over to bus operation on 19th April 1931, but while the conversions took place smoothly, running trams to Broad Lane could only be a short-term solution.

By the end of 1931 the trams were fast disappearing from the streets of Rochdale. In the picture above, taken from the upper floor of the Wellington Hotel, two Dennis and three lowbridge Crossleys circle the town centre while in the background a solitary tram can be seen on the Manchester route. *(RLS)*

In the lower picture taken in October 1932, number 107, a recently delivered English Electric highbridge bodied Crossley Condor, stands outside the Transport Offices in Mellor Street, together with number 80, a seven-year-old English Electric tramcar which it was shortly to replace on the Manchester route, thus bringing the tramway era to an end. *(RLS)*

It was now becoming increasingly clear that the total abandonment of the tramway system was the only option. In February 1931 Mr Edwards recommended conversion of the Bacup, Heywood and Milnrow Road routes, leaving only the Manchester route still operated by trams. The Bacup service was chosen for the first stage and a further twelve double-deck buses were ordered. Nine were Crossley Condors, the first three with petrol engines and the remainder with oil engines, these latter also being fitted with Crossley's 'automatic gear changing device'. The rest of the order was for Dennis Lances with English Electric bodies. These had left hand gear change levers, the first in the fleet. All were said to be of the 'conventional' type, which was Rochdale's description for a normal height body rather than a lowbridge one. They arrived late in 1931, the Crossleys numbered 70-8 (DK7480-8), and the Dennises 79-81 (DK7489-91).

In July Crossley asked if they could exhibit a bus in the Rochdale colour scheme on their stand at the Commercial Motor Show later in the year. Rochdale agreed and again they decided to purchase the vehicle, a diesel-engined Condor which became 82 (DK7646), arriving in February 1932.

Conversion of the Bacup service was not a simple matter, as it was necessary to obtain powers to abandon the tracks beyond the Borough boundary in Whitworth and Bacup. In the meantime, it was decided to retain some peak period and Saturday tram operation in order to comply with the terms of the 1925 Act, and use the rest of the buses to complete the conversion of the Oldham Road route.

The position in Milnrow was similar so another twelve buses were ordered to convert the bulk of the Newhay route while still running a token tram service until the necessary powers were obtained. These were more Crossley Condors numbered 83-94 (DK7861-72).

The Bacup tram service ceased on 14th May 1932, buses taking over the following day. On the same day the Bacup to Manchester express bus was withdrawn, and the partial replacement of the Newhay service was implemented, with the full conversion taking place on 7th August 1932.

Negotiations with Heywood Council were more protracted. Heywood had built and owned the lines in the Borough, but did not lease them to Rochdale, as did Littleborough, Wardle and Milnrow. Instead, they allowed Rochdale, Bury and Manchester to run over their lines, paying a proportion of the working expenses and taking a share in the revenue. Rochdale and Bury offered to pay Heywood £9,000, which was the outstanding capital on the tramway within the Borough. Heywood, however, insisted that they should also be paid for re-instating the road. The view taken by Rochdale and Bury was that, as the lines were owned by Heywood and had never been leased to them, this was Heywood's responsibility.

With the Road Traffic Act on the horizon negotiations were suspended, and when the Act became law Rochdale and Bury offered to run the bus service, take the receipts and pay the expenses. Heywood, however, faced with the cost of highway re-instatement with no income to offset it, demanded a share of the receipts, similar to the arrangements which existed on the Rochdale-Bolton express service.

More talks took place but by the end of October 1931 an impasse was reached. Heywood decided that they would do better running their own buses and applied to the newly formed Traffic Commissioners for consent. Rochdale and Bury objected and finally, on 13th June 1932 the Commissioners refused Heywood's application. The three Corporations subsequently reached agreement and at last buses took over from the trams on 3rd July 1932..

IT WASN'T ME GUV

In June 1931 the Passenger Transport Committee decided to write to the Chief Constable of Lancashire protesting against the action of the police in detaining one of their bus drivers. It was alleged that the driver in question entered a house in Norden for a perfectly innocent purpose and found that the police were conducting a betting raid. He was detained and taken to the police station, although he was not charged. The Committee's complaint was that the police had not notified the Transport Department and that consequently the bus service was seriously disrupted.

The Chief Constable was unsympathetic and the Committee decided not to take the matter further.

THE END OF THE LINE

In May 1932 the Passenger Transport Committee agreed to order a further 23 buses to replace the remaining trams. These were all oil-engined Crossley Condors. The body order was split with the first ten going to Crossley and the other 13 to English Electric. They were all normal height bodies and were to be numbered 95-117 (DK7980-3, 8014-32).

Now, only the Manchester tram service remained, the conversion of which had been agreed in April 1932. However, Manchester was overstretched for buses and in August wrote to Rochdale saying that it would not be possible to run the substitute bus service before the beginning of October. This final conversion did not go in easily. The proposed 10-minute headway was to replace both the express bus and the tram service, but because the Road Traffic Act did not cover trams, the application was technically for an increase in the frequency of the existing bus service and the introduction of tramway fares on it. This provoked objections from Yelloway on the grounds that any greater frequency on the Corporation's route would be detrimental to its own service, and by the LMS Railway because of the lower fares proposed.

The Traffic Commissioners convened a hearing at Manchester Town Hall on 2nd November and granted the application on condition that the existing tram fares should be charged within Rochdale, but that the through fares between Rochdale and Manchester should not undercut those of Yelloway. The new service commenced on 13th November 1932.

So, a little over six years after the first Corporation bus service started to run to Castleton, trams had disappeared from the streets of Rochdale. The motorbus era had begun.

Trams no more. In the upper picture Crossley 71 leaves the Tramway Centre for Broad Lane. Note the route number in the upper deck window and the metal plate which has replaced the destination blind. *(JHC)*

In the picture below the tracks are still in place as Crossley 40 rolls along a traffic-free Esplanade with the Post Office on the left and the Town Hall on the right. *(RLS)*

THE ROAD TRAFFIC ACT 1930

The main purpose of Herbert Morrison's Road Traffic Act was to streamline the licensing procedure by taking it away from the multitude of local authorities, each with its own independent transport policy, and concentrating it into a number of Traffic Areas presided over by Government appointed Traffic Commissioners. The intention was to simplify the process and bring consistency to the decision-making. So far as the passenger industry was concerned it covered the issue and renewal of Road Service Licences, Public Service Vehicle Licences and Driver and Conductor Licences. Trams, and trolley buses, which were considered to be a type of tram, were not covered by the regulations. Rochdale came within the North Western Traffic Area with its headquarters at Sunlight House in Manchester, the Chairman of the Commissioners being William (later Sir William) Chamberlain who at one time had been General Manager of the Oldham Corporation Transport Department.

All existing operators had to apply for licences to continue the services they were already running. However, transitional regulations were issued on 9th February 1931 under which all vehicles and services operating on that date were allowed to continue running subject to any conditions then in force, until such time as the applications for licences could be heard and determined. The Minister of Transport made it clear, however, that permission to continue an existing service did not carry with it any rights, and the Traffic Commissioners would not be placed under any obligation when they came to consider the grant of the substantive licence for these services.

Established bodies, such as local authorities, other operators and the railway companies, were able to object to applications, even if the services had been running for a considerable time, although they would have to put up convincing arguments in support of their objections. Generally, town services operated by the local councils continued unchallenged. The majority of objections were against the longer distance inter-town services, particularly the expresses, where the railway companies seized the opportunity to reopen old

The disused tram tracks are still in place in this 1932 view of the Esplanade as a Ribble Leyland Lion follows a sports car across the junction with Manchester Road on its way to Burnley. The area is little changed today, the ornate building on the left now housing the art gallery, museum and local studies library, while mature trees occupy the slopes of Broadfield Park on the right. The once heavily loaded service over Owd Betts to Edenfield and beyond no longer operates. *(RLS)*

Not a tram in sight. Buses only in this view of the south end of Mellor Street depot in 1933. *(MMT)*

arguments and get a second bite at the cherry. In addition there was growing concern over traffic congestion, particularly in Manchester city centre, which the railways and the taxi operators exploited in a bid to get the express services withdrawn.

Amongst the first applications to be considered were Rochdale's express services between Littleborough and Altrincham, and between Bacup and Flixton, jointly operated with Manchester. On 11th May 1931, five days before the Hearing, the LMS Railway had re-opened its newly electrified line between Manchester and Altrincham, which paralleled the bus route for most of its length.

The railway fought tooth and nail to protect its investment, suggesting that the bus services should be withdrawn and run as feeders to the railway stations. The Commissioners accepted the railway case in part and decreed that both express services should be withdrawn south of Manchester, and terminate on the edge of the city centre. They were cut back to operate between Littleborough or Bacup and Manchester (Cannon Street) from 19th July 1931.

Manchester's service between Norden and Gatley, which had been the first of the express services dating from April 1927, also fell foul of the new regime. The railway's objections were disallowed as they only ran a minimal service

between Heywood and Manchester on an indirect route, but the complaint of congestion was upheld, and like many other cross-Manchester services it was split in the city centre from 25th October 1931. Rochdale were also instructed to split the Littleborough service in the town centre, so from 15th November 1931 the express buses reverted to their original route between Rochdale and Manchester with the Littleborough section incorporated into the existing local service.

The LMS also objected to the express services from Rochdale to Bolton, Ashton and Todmorden, but here the Commissioners turned down the objections. On the other hand the LMS service between Rochdale and Halifax, once so contentious, was confirmed.

A service from Rochdale to Birch Hill Hospital, on visiting days, commenced on 11th November.

There was one last confrontation with the railways before things settled down. In June 1932 Rochdale, among others, objected unsuccessfully to the LMS application for a Road Service Licence to provide a service of stage carriages between any two points served by an advertised train service on their system when, owing to emergencies or events beyond the Company's control, the rail service was interrupted. This was the origin of rail replacement services.

A PERIOD OF CONSOLIDATION

The end of 1932 saw the culmination of an eventful six years that had started with the first motorbuses, seen the rise and fall of the express services and the abandonment of the entire tramway network. The bus fleet now stood at 114, of which 48 were single-deckers. Of the 66 double-deckers 43 had diesel engines, thirty-five were less than one year old, and the fleet was set to remain unchanged until the first of the Dennis single-deckers became due for replacement.

The network was now complete and the Rochdale Official Handbook waxed lyrical.

"The town is possessed of excellent passenger transport services and it is possible to get from one outlying district to another very quickly by motor omnibuses. These omnibuses run to and from Rochdale and Manchester every quarter of an hour, and there are 10-minute services to and from Littleborough, Whitworth, Newhey, Milnrow, Norden and Thornham. There are also regular services to Bacup, Bolton, Bury, Oldham, Ashton and Todmorden. The services also cover all the new housing areas and every route starts in the centre of the town."

This was praise indeed, and a self-congratulatory pat on the back.

So, after the frenetic activity of the past few years, it was time to take stock of the situation. Abandoning the trams had come at a huge cost in capital expenditure and highway reinstatement and to compound this, traffic and revenue had fallen due to the economic depression. In the half-year ending 30th September 1932 there had been a net deficit of £6,777, and although the loss-making tramway operation would soon cease to exist there were still outstanding debts that would have to be paid off for a number of years to come.

Some of the conversions had been done on the cheap with extremely tight running times to keep the bus and crew requirements to a minimum. The Bury service was given the same time end to end as the express bus over the same section of route, which had only a quarter of the stops. There were stories of drivers doing 45 mph on the rural section between Heywood and Marland to make up lost time, although with an oil-engined Crossley Condor on the roads of that period this seems something of an exaggeration. It would certainly have been exciting.

The Bacup route was little better, its running time of 31 minutes being only one more than the express bus it had replaced. Complaints of late running and bunching were numerous, so much so that Whitworth Council briefly considered

Drake Street at its junction with Oldham Road early in 1933, the spot where a little over 50 years previously the first paving sett was lifted to commence construction of the steam tramway. A lowbridge Condor climbs the hill on its way to Manchester. *(RLS)*

A stray dog watches the photographer in this atmospheric 1933 view of a foggy Smith Street. On the left a Dennis and a highbridge Condor wait for custom, while another Dennis can be seen on the right. *(RLS)*

operating its own buses. However, a closer look at the costs involved convinced them that they were better off having Rochdale to blame rather than taking responsibility themselves.

Meanwhile, there had been complaints about the narrow part of Heights Lane on the Syke route. When two buses collided there the route was changed to Hope Street and Whitehall Street, which had the added advantage of passing the main entrance to the Infirmary. The residents of Lanehead once again asked for a service, but the Department still considered the road unfit.

Construction of the reservoirs on Blackstone Edge was now complete and by the end of 1931 the remaining traffic could be carried by the LMS Halifax buses. It was first proposed to reduce the service to early morning and workmen's journeys operating only as far as the Moorcock Inn for the local mills, but it was later decided to withdraw the service altogether and it came off in September 1932. Littleborough Council, who had fought long and hard to get the service in the first place, made repeated representations over the next two

years to reinstate some workmen's journeys, but to no avail.

By now Manchester Corporation was becoming concerned at the loss of traffic on the service between Norden and Manchester, which had been extended from Heywood some four years previously, largely to fill a gap which might be exploited by a competitor. On 24th October the service was curtailed at the Heywood boundary at Hall Gates and reduced to hourly, Norden and Bamford being served by a supplementary service between Heywood and Norden. Rochdale were quite happy as by then they were running their Bamford Circular which took passengers to work and shop in Rochdale rather than in Heywood and which to a great extent had contributed to the situation. Then on 19th July 1933 the Manchester service was reinstated as far as Bamford Village and the Heywood to Norden shuttle was withdrawn.

The Bury Road service (1) was extended in stages to Woodlands Avenue, The Elephant and Castle and eventually Wood Top Drive.

THE BUS STATION FURORE

Towards the end of 1932 another matter was generating a lot of interest in the town. The tram services had all terminated around a large island in the middle of the town centre, then known as the Broadway, which contained waiting rooms and an inspectors' office. However, the replacement buses needed room to turn round, resulting in conflicting manoeuvres. With traffic congestion now becoming an issue, the Borough Surveyor drew up plans to remove the former Tramway Centre and replace it with a traffic island the length of the Broadway, converting it into two parallel one-way streets and relocating the bus stands to the pavements on either side.

The work needed to be started urgently as the money was coming from the Government's First Class Roads Fund, which provided grants for improving major roads, of which the A58 through the town centre was one, and if a start was not made soon the money would be lost. But, while in general the plan was welcomed, the Council, divided on the detail, deferred a decision and called for expert opinion on the proposal.

The expert invited by the Corporation was Sir Henry Maybury, soon to become Lord Maybury, who up to his recent retirement had enjoyed considerable prominence as a road engineer, latterly holding the position of Director of Roads in the Ministry of Transport. Sir Henry visited Rochdale at the end of May 1933 and toured the town centre with leading officials and politicians. Six days later he produced a report that backed up the Council's scheme, but went further and recommended building a bus station on the Town Hall Square. Unfortunately, it also required the removal of John Bright's statue from its position in the square.

John Bright was one of Rochdale's favourite sons. Born in the Borough in 1811 he became the town's Member of Parliament and a Government Minister, his chief claims to fame being the repeal of the Corn Laws and the introduction of the Reform Act of 1867, which had extended the vote to working men. He was something of a folk hero in the town.

This was a step too far. The people of Rochdale were proud of their town centre, especially their magnificent Town Hall and its surroundings, and when Sir Henry's report was published there was a public outcry. Despite this, the Paving Committee passed the proposal, which was then endorsed by the chairmen of the other interested committees, and a wooden mock-up of the bus station was laid out on the Town Hall Square while trials were conducted.

When the Bright statue was removed from its plinth towards the end of June, public anger boiled over and a protest meeting was called in the Town Hall. Twenty minutes before the advertised time the hall was packed, with hundreds of people unable to get in, and arrangements were quickly made for an overflow meeting to take place on the nearby Cattle Market, attended by an estimated 2,000 people. Both meetings unanimously passed a resolution denouncing the scheme as a piece of vandalism and called on the Council to abandon it.

Faced with such strength of opposition the Council, at its July meeting, decided to stop the work for further discussions to take place. A month later they resolved to go ahead with the demolition of the tramway island, but not to proceed with the bus station. Instead, the Passenger Transport Committee was instructed to prepare an alternative plan. People power had triumphed, but the outcome was basically a modified version of the Borough Surveyor's original scheme for pavement stands. When it was implemented passengers changing buses would find that they could have a lengthy walk across the town centre, which, in the depths of a Lancashire winter, was not what they had envisaged. The arguments and recriminations rumbled on for many months, but with some minor changes the revised stopping places stood the test of time until the question of a bus station again reared its head in the post-war Rochdale Town Plan.

INTERESTING TIMES

There is an old Chinese curse, which says, *"May you live in interesting times"*, interesting perhaps for the historian but not much fun for those living through them. Such a period was the 1930s with its trade depression, mass unemployment and political unrest culminating in the Second World War. Although the bus station issue had dominated much of 1933 and the early part of 1934, it was merely a

The town centre in 1933 photographed from the Town Hall. The former tramway centre is in the foreground and any traffic congestion in the area would seem to be caused by the buses, which far outnumber other vehicles. *(RLS)*

Pictured at a site meeting to discuss the proposed new bus station are, from left to right, Passenger Transport Manager Mr George Webster, Chairman of the Passenger Transport Committee Alderman Clark JP, Councillor Crossley, Sir Henry Maybury, Chairman of the General Purposes Committee Alderman Bryning, Chairman of the Paving Committee Councillor Parker, Borough Surveyor Mr SH Morgan and Town Clerk Mr WH Hickson. *(RO)*

diversion from the very real problems of rising costs and falling passenger levels.

With a fares increase politically unacceptable, the only course of action was service economies and Mr Edwards drew up a scheme largely consisting of reductions in frequency, but also including two more contentious proposals. These were the withdrawal of all the Littleborough local services and the Rochdale to Todmorden express bus, the latter to be replaced by a through local service incorporating the existing routes either side of Littleborough Summit.

Littleborough Council, still smarting from the withdrawal of the Blackstone Edge service, and feeling that they were being singled out unfairly, protested to the Traffic Commissioners. At a Hearing in Rochdale Town Hall on 30th October 1934 they contended that the local services in the town should not be considered in isolation, and as they had actively supported Rochdale in creating

a monopoly, Rochdale had a duty to provide an adequate service to the people of Littleborough. Rochdale's case was that it was not right that the ratepayers of Rochdale should pay for losses on a service outside the Borough.

Having pointed out that there was, in fact, nothing to prevent Rochdale from withdrawing the services and returning the licences for cancellation, the Commissioners considered that they themselves might also be expected to have some views on the matter and had decided to hold an Enquiry to hear both sides of the argument. They had sympathy with Littleborough's position, and considered the losses on the services to be a small part of the whole problem. Figures were important, but there were also hidden costs and it was often better to provide a service at a small loss as, if it were to be withdrawn, all the revenue would be lost and most of the costs would simply be transferred elsewhere. Compared to many

By the beginning of 1935 the earlier Dennis vehicles were becoming due for replacement and since the tried and trusted Crossley Condor was no longer available two Crossley Mancunians were ordered similar to buses already in service in Manchester and which were already working into Rochdale on the jointly operated service 17. At the same time two AEC Regents, a type new to Rochdale, were ordered for evaluation. Number 118, the first of the Crossleys, is pictured on the Esplanade near the General Post Office about 1947, shortly before withdrawal. AEC 120, the first new bus to carry the blue livery, is standing behind. *(PDC)*

operators within the North Western traffic area, Rochdale were in a very good position, and the Commissioners said they would like to feel that Rochdale would continue to be a fairy godmother and not regard Littleborough as their Cinderella.

Suitably chastised, Rochdale accepted the Commissioners' recommendation and continued to operate the services. They also withdrew the proposal for the Todmorden route and, with 1935 showing signs of an upturn in trade most of the cuts in frequency were reinstated.

DIESEL VERSUS PETROL

Since the introduction of the first diesel Condors there had been a long running argument about the relative merits of petrol and oil engines. There was a great debate in Council and in the local press on the subject, but with several years experience of running diesel buses, it was decided to fit 16 of the newer Dennis petrol single-deckers, numbers 20-35 with standard Crossley oil engines. Number 36, the show model, was never converted and remained the only petrol-engined Dennis single-decker in the fleet, outlasting all the diesel buses.

As the earlier Dennisses were becoming due for replacement, four new double-deck buses were ordered at the beginning of 1935. Of these, two were Crossley Mancunian double-deckers with bodies to the latest Manchester design constructed by Crossley on Metro-Cammell metal frames, which would be 118-9 (ADK78-9) when delivered. The other two were to be a new departure for the Corporation; AEC Regents with standard Metro-Cammell bodies and pre-selector gearboxes with fluid flywheels, numbered 120-1 (ADK282-3). These four buses re-introduced roller blind indicators to the Rochdale fleet. They were ordered for evaluation as production of the Crossley Condor had now ceased, but the choice of the two AECs again provoked arguments against non-standard buses. When they arrived later in the year they replaced Dennisses 4, 13 and 15 and accident damaged Condor 66, 4 becoming a towing vehicle.

From the beginning Rochdale's buses had been painted, like the trams, in a dignified brown and deep cream, sometimes described as yellow. By 1935, however, this was beginning to look old fashioned and out of tune with the modern, progressive image that the department wanted to project. So it was decided to try out different colour schemes and eight Condors were chosen for the experiment; 41 and 42 were painted in a lighter shade of brown, 53, 54 and 115 in a somewhat daring red, yellow and cream and 39, 64 and 109 in blue and cream. The blue was chosen and the first new buses to carry it were the two AECs, 120 and 121. The existing fleet was steadily repainted and the old metal plate destination indicators were replaced by roller blinds. All the fleet had been modernised by the summer of 1936 and some of the repainted buses had their seats re-trimmed in blue and the interiors repainted in blue and white with light oak woodwork, a policy which was to be continued on all later orders.

THE SELEC SCHEME

Meanwhile, another matter was exercising the minds of the Transport Committee. Within the Manchester area there had long been a high degree of co-ordination and joint working of services between the various operators, both municipal and company, dating back to the early tramway days. After the demise of the abortive Joint Control Committee comprising municipal undertakings either side of the Pennines, Rochdale had become involved in the great express network and by this time was running joint services with six other municipal operators as well as the North Western Road Car Company.

Following the implementation of the 1930 Road Traffic Act, discussions had been taking place on the subject of a Joint Municipal Passenger Transport Board for South East Lancashire and East Cheshire, known as SELEC, the brainchild of Manchester's General Manager, R Stuart Pilcher. In 1931 representatives of Ashton, Bolton, Bury, Leigh, Manchester, Oldham, Rochdale, Salford, SHMD, Stockport and Wigan had met to discuss broad principles of a merger. Leigh and Wigan soon withdrew as they had little common interest with the rest of the group, but Manchester continued to host a series of conferences.

There were, however, two main stumbling blocks to agreement; fears of the loss of local influence over services and fares, and worries about how the different outstanding capital debts would be treated. One by one operators withdrew and by 1935 only Rochdale, together with Manchester, Oldham and Salford, were still interested. Rochdale's view was that the scheme could do the same for South Lancashire as the creation of the London Passenger Transport Board two years previously had done for London, and also, unless a voluntary arrangement was reached, the Government might impose a less advantageous compulsory scheme upon them. Nonetheless, although still committed to the principle, Rochdale could not accept the detail and withdrew from the scheme in the April. A meeting of the three remaining operators took place on 17th July 1935 when it was decided not to promote the necessary Bill.

Nothing more came of the idea, although a final conference of all the municipal operators, plus Ribble, North Western and Lancashire United, took place the following year, and it was not for another 34 years that the 1968 Transport Act would create the Passenger Transport Authorities and Rochdale Corporation Transport would be no more.

UNDER NEW MANAGEMENT

In January 1936 the transport world was rocked by the news that George Edwards, Rochdale's General Manager, had died after a short illness. Mr Edwards had been born in the town, attended the local grammar school and after a short time in the family business had joined the Bury, Rochdale and Oldham Steam Tramway Company in 1891, rising to the position of Traffic Manager. When the Corporation took over the company's operations in the town in 1904, he was appointed to a similar position in the extended municipal system, being very much involved in the creation and organisation of the Corporation's new electric network. In 1913 he succeeded Mr JSD Moffett as General Manager and for his last 23 years had overseen the introduction of the motorbus, the rise and fall of the express network and the eventual demise of the tramways. Mr Edwards was awarded the OBE for his wartime services and had spent a total of 45 years in the industry.

Mr Edwards' successor as General Manager was George Arnold Cherry, the Assistant

Mr. George Edwards OBE, General Manager from 1913 to 1936. (*RO*)

Manager and Engineer of Kingston upon Hull Corporation. A tough Yorkshireman from Sheffield, he had served an apprenticeship in mechanical engineering before joining the Royal Army Service Corps, rising to the rank of Sergeant Major in charge of a transport unit on the North West Frontier. On leaving the army in 1923 he joined the Yorkshire Traction Company as Assistant Engineer, later becoming Assistant Rolling Stock Engineer and then Deputy Manager and Engineer at Rotherham Corporation before taking up his current position at Hull.

Mr Cherry's first challenge was to bring down the labour costs of the engineering section. His target was the night shift in the depot, always the least efficient of operations, and by reorganising this he was able to dispense with 14 men, most of who were well past normal retiring age. Mr Edwards had been known as a strict disciplinarian, but a fair man who looked after his staff, and there is little doubt that he had created light jobs for those least able to fend for themselves. The men's union was incensed and threatened to strike unless the men were reinstated and eventually the Ministry of Transport's Chief Conciliation Officer was called in. The Union proposed a temporary reduction in hours and job sharing, and eventually an agreement was reached.

For the past six years neighbouring Manchester Corporation had been steadily converting its tramway system to diesel buses. However, during this time considerable advances had been made in the technology of the third alternative, the trackless trolley vehicle or trolley bus, and with mass unemployment there was a growing lobby for the use of home produced electricity for traction instead of imported oil.

The ensuing power struggle within Manchester City Council has been well documented but suffice to say that the trolley bus faction won the day and a Bill was deposited with Parliament early in 1936 seeking powers to operate trolley buses. This would not have concerned Rochdale, except for two clauses in the Bill, to run trolley buses on any public road in or outside the city, and to generate the necessary electricity. As the Town Clerk observed, it would be theoretically possible for Manchester to run trolley buses to Land's End, and there was a whiff of hypocrisy in the Council's decision to object to clauses which they themselves had fought successfully to include in their own Rochdale Corporation Act eleven years earlier.

However, with most other municipalities in the area raising similar objections, protective clauses were negotiated and the Bill went through unopposed in the May. Trolley buses never came to Rochdale and the motorbus reigned supreme until the end.

Two orders for new buses were placed during 1936. The first, early in the year, was for six AEC Regents with pre-selector gearboxes and two Leyland TD4s with torque converters designated TD4c. The torque converter provided a fully automatic transmission apart from a manually engaged direct drive that was the equivalent of the top gear. It was controlled by a selector lever replacing the normal gear lever, with four positions, converter, direct, neutral and reverse. There was no clutch pedal. The converter was used for all conditions, from stationary where it acted in the same way as a centrifugal clutch, up to top gear speeds when the direct drive was selected. When starting from rest the engine speed would rise to around 1,200 rpm. and then remain

While George Edwards had gone for a policy of standardisation, his successor Arnold Cherry went the other way, splitting both chassis and body orders two or even three ways. The first bus delivered during his reign as General Manager was 122, one of a trio of English Electric-bodied AEC Regents pictured on the Smith Street bus park in the early fifties. *(RM)*

Number 126 was one of a pair of Regents with Weymann bodies. Companions 128 and 129, which completed the 1936 order, had identical bodies on Leyland Titan TD4 chassis fitted with torque converters. *(STA)*

constant as the bus accelerated, the converter acting as an infinitely variable drive up to about 20 mph. when the direct drive was engaged. The torque converter did away with the need for the driver to change gear and some operators took large numbers of these vehicles for tramway conversions, considering it easier to train former tram drivers on them rather than on buses with a conventional clutch and crash gearbox. Rochdale, with no tram drivers left to retrain, was more concerned with the downside of lower power and higher fuel consumption and, apart from five more examples delivered in 1938, showed no further interest.

The four Regents with English Electric bodies, numbered 122-5 (BDK207-10) were delivered in the late summer, while the remaining Regents and the two Leylands with Weymann bodies numbered 126-9 (BDK353-6) arrived before the end of the year.

Later in the year ten more buses were ordered, five Leyland TS7 single-deckers and five more AEC Regents, this time bodied by Cravens of Sheffield, a company new to the Corporation, although not to its General Manager. They were delivered in April 1937 and were numbered 130-9 (CDK204-13). These two batches, with one exception, replaced the last of the petrol-engined Dennises, leaving only those that had been fitted with Crossley oil engines. The one remaining petrol-engined Dennis was 36, the Commercial Motor Show model that retained its petrol engine until the end. No more Crossleys were to be ordered. These buses introduced the revised livery incorporating a downward swoop in the blue that left the front of the bus completely cream.

The Department's finances had started to turn the corner, and in the 1936/7 financial year, it made a profit for the first time since 1930. While some of it had come from a reduction in working expenses, much of the surplus was due to the fall in interest charges owing to the paying off of loans on the abandoned tramways. The net profit of £6,196 was used to offset the previous year's loss and to pay off the loan borrowed for the conversion of 16 of the petrol-engined Dennises to diesel. There were still problems ahead, however, with projected increases in the price of fuel and licences.

For 1937 another new body builder was specified, this time Cravens of Sheffield. The order was split, the first five being Leyland Tiger TS7s. Number 130 is pictured standing at the back of Mellor Street depot yard after being re-numbered 1 in 1939. *(PDC)*

The other five buses were more Regents. Number 136 stands behind the Town Hall displaying the revised livery with the front swoops. This picture was also used for Cravens' adverts. *(MMT)*

For a week in May 1937 an illuminated bus toured the Borough to celebrate the Coronation of King George VI and Queen Elizabeth. This was the first such occasion since the demise of the trams and the tableau was scaled down to preserve the batteries. Nevertheless, hundreds of people turned out to see the spectacle.

PROBLEMS

Mr Cherry, in an address to the Insurance Institute in Manchester in July 1937, set out the problems facing the public transport industry in general, and Rochdale in particular.

First, he said that there was the difficulty of peak hour loadings. Rochdale currently operated a fleet of 126 buses, the average number required for regular service being 86. However, between 5.15pm and 6.15pm they turned out a total of 124, meaning that 38 buses, or nearly a third of the fleet, were only used for an hour and a half every day. If evening finishing times at the factories and mills were to be staggered by as little as 15 minutes, then it would free twelve buses to reduce peak period waiting times in other areas. However, there had been little enthusiasm for such a policy with either the employers or the trades unions.

Secondly, there was increasing congestion in the town centre. In Rochdale it was no uncommon thing for cars to be parked on bus stops, preventing the drivers from drawing their buses up to the kerb edge and blocking the flow of traffic while passengers alighted and boarded. It had been suggested that a bus station should be constructed on the edge of the town centre, but the buses were carrying three million passengers a year and their views should be considered before those of a handful of motorists. It had also been found that a remote bus station would have an adverse effect on the number of passengers riding short stages, as, if they had to walk to a bus station, they would often walk the rest of the way.

The third problem had been created by the rehousing of people from the very congested central areas, often at a considerable distance from their work. Very often the rehousing caused a definite hardship because people were asked to pay more rent and pressure was brought to bear on the Transport Department to reduce its fares to offset this. Mr Cherry contended that where people were rehoused as a social amenity and in the interests of public health, then the responsibility should lie with the committee that had insisted on the people being rehoused. There was no reason why they should be carried at an uneconomic fare when the Transport Department was expected to be a self –supporting business concern.

A last, but very important, point was the cheap return fares for workmen that had been going on for many years. While the workmen's fare was an admirable institution for the workman, there was no other commodity where the workman got a preferential price. Workmen's fares had the effect of increasing the fares for the rest of the passengers.

Much of this was forward thinking for the time and Mr Cherry rounded off his talk by commenting that if only one more passenger could be attracted to the buses for every two miles run, then that would mean additional revenue of £8,000 a year.

The 1937 order for new buses again broke new ground. It consisted of twelve Leyland TD5s, five with torque converters, and five Daimler COG6s with pre-selector gearboxes. Twelve were bodied by Cravens, but the five crash-box Leylands were bodied by Eastern Counties of Lowestoft, who had bid unsuccessfully for the previous order. All were delivered in April 1938 and were numbered 140-56 (DDK110-26). The new buses replaced 15 of the early petrol-engined lowbridge Crossleys. The latter were still only eight years old, but their timber-framed bodies had deteriorated to the point where it was uneconomical to repair them.

Meanwhile, the Department was experimenting with ticket machines. Two TIM machines, printing on plain paper rolls, were placed in service for three months. They were said to be quicker than the current Bell Punch system and speeded up fares collection at peak periods, there was less waybill work, and the plain rolls were a third of the price of the existing pre-printed tickets. However, no more were purchased and the Bell Punch tickets continued in use for many years to come.

On 6th November 1937 Oldham Corporation abandoned its trams between Thornham and Hathershaw and the following day a 10-minute local service (9) started running between Rochdale and Hathershaw, connecting there with Ashton's trolley buses. As a result the Thornham to Norden service (9A/9C) was split in the town centre with

The 1938 deliveries totalled 17 buses, comprising various combinations of Leyland and Daimler chassis and Cravens and Eastern Coach Works bodies, the latter a builder new to Rochdale. Number 141, a Leyland Titan TD5c with torque converter and Cravens 54-seat body, had gained a crash gearbox, Manchester style destination indicators and increased seating by the time the photograph was taken. *(PDC)*

Number 148, pictured on the Smith Street bus park in the early fifties, had a crash box from new and carried this 56-seat body by ECW of Lowestoft. *(PDC)*

The last four buses were Daimler COG6s, yet another new departure for Rochdale. They were fitted with Cravens bodies identical to those of 140-4, that on 154, standing on Packer Street before leaving for Bamford Village on service 5, is displaying the original design of destination indicators. *(RM)*

a peak hour Bagslate to Broad Lane service (9B) providing a limited cross town facility. Public pressure soon saw it reinstated.

April 1938 saw the death of Alderman Harry Clark, the Chairman of the Passenger Transport Committee. A native of Rushden in Northamptonshire, he had come to Rochdale 50 years previously and set up in the footwear business. A Councillor since 1902, he became Mayor in 1920, an Alderman in 1923 and Chairman of the Tramways Committee two years later. Together with the late General Manager, George Webster, he had driven through the introduction of the first motorbuses and the final demise of the trams. A forthright character, he revelled in controversy and had often said that he was more comfortable when people were criticising him than praising him, as at least it showed he was doing something.

Alderman Clark. *(RO)*

THE GATHERING STORM

At the end of the 1936/7 financial year the Passenger Transport Department had made a profit of just over £6,000. The Committee had resisted calls to reduce fares and instead had used the money to pay off some of the capital debt, but had promised to look at a fares reduction the following year if a similar profit were to be made. By the end of 1937 it was becoming apparent that there would indeed be a substantial profit and the General Manager was asked to report on how this money might be spent.

Mr Cherry recommended reductions of a halfpenny on longer distance journeys on the Newhay (3/6), Littleborough (3/6), Wardle (4), Syke (10) and Spotland (12) routes where the fare per mile was higher than elsewhere on the system, together with some alterations to stages on the Castleton (1) and Bacup (16) routes. No change was recommended on any of the other routes. The annual cost of this was anticipated to be £4,000.

On the question of workmen's fares, although Rochdale were giving better value than they were called upon to do under the 1930 Act, and indeed were offering better conditions than most other municipalities in the North Western Traffic Area, no action was recommended for the time being. Instead Mr Cherry proposed to use any remaining surplus on capital expenditure, especially the provision of passenger shelters. The report was approved and passed by the Council on 5th May.

The new fares came into force on 24th May 1938 with the exception of those on the Littleborough services, which were subject to an objection from Todmorden Council because of their effect on the express bus. On the same day the route of the Spotland service was changed to cater for the expanding Brotherod and Spotland housing estates. Since the end of tramway operation most buses had turned at the junction of Rooley Moor Road and Ings Lane, with some journeys extending to Brookside and a few to Lanehead. The route was diverted up Ings Lane to Daniel Fold with some journeys turning short at Brotherod Hall Road.

The 1938 order for new buses consisted of ten double-deckers and eight single-deckers. The double-deckers were five AEC Regents with ECW bodies numbered 157-61 (DDK832-6) and five Leyland TD5s with Weymann bodies numbered 162-6 (DDK918-22). The single-deckers were Leyland TS8s with ECW bodies numbered 6-13 (EDK101-8), following on from 1937 Leyland TS7s 130-4 which had become 1-5. They arrived in May 1939 and replaced more Dennises and Crossleys including the three Dennis Lance

Eighteen new buses were delivered in 1939, again comprising combinations of AEC and Leyland chassis with Weymann or Eastern Coach Works bodies.

Number 158, an AEC Regent with Eastern Coach Works 56-seat body, stands on South Parade on service 10 to Syke. *(JHC)*

Number 162, seen working a football special in the early fifties, was a Leyland TD5 with a 56-seat body built by Weymann. *(JHC)*

Eight buses were Leyland TS8 single-deckers with Eastern Coach Works 36-seat bodies. Number 12 poses for its official maker's photograph at Oulton Broad before leaving for Rochdale. *(STA)*

double-deckers 79-81. All had saloon heaters, being the first Rochdale buses so fitted. The Committee had considered fitting some of the older buses with heaters, but having discovered that the extra weight would take the buses over the permitted limit, decided not to do so.

On 18th February 1939 Ashton Corporation withdrew their trolley bus service between Ashton and Hathershaw and on the following day the Rochdale to Hathershaw service (9) was extended to Ashton in its place. At the same time the Rochdale to Ashton express service (7) came off, leaving just a 10-minute local service throughout.

In the financial year ending 31st March 1939 the Department made an operating surplus of £31,000. The capital debt on tramway abandonment had been steadily reducing, but repayment charges were still £14,000 a year and provision had now to be made for the new superannuation scheme and holidays with pay that had just been agreed nationally. When this had been taken into account it was possible for £7,000 to be transferred to the general rate fund, the first time this had been done since 1930 before the start of tramway abandonment.

As 1939 rolled on, the political situation in Europe worsened, and preparations were made for the inevitable outbreak of war with Germany. Air raid shelters were erected on the old cattle market, training was given on how to deal with unexploded bombs and blackout exercises were carried out. In July the Traffic Commissioners asked Rochdale to be prepared to provide transport for approximately 3,500 people who might need to be evacuated from Manchester to Littleborough, Wardle and Whitworth.

A request was also made for the bus shelter and waiting room at Sudden to be used as an ARP post and an office for the senior warden for the area. The committee agreed on the condition that public access to the toilets was maintained. There might be a war looming, but there were other priorities as well.

On 1st September German tanks rolled into Poland and two days later Britain declared war on Germany. The Second World War had begun.

Very little traffic can be seen in this picture of Mellor Street in the summer of 1939 as an ECW-bodied Leyland TD5 heads into town from the depot and approaches the bridge over the River Roch. (*RLS*)

ROCHDALE AT WAR

With the outbreak of war, regulation of transport came under the newly created Ministry of War Transport and was administered by the former Chairmen of the Area Traffic Commissioners who became Regional Traffic Commissioners, the Commissioner for the North Western Region being Sir William Chamberlain.

Now that hostilities had commenced, things started to happen quickly. With a blackout imposed, side and rear lights were masked and the offside headlamp removed. Interior saloon lighting was reduced and the front mudguards and rear corners of the buses were painted white. White lines were also painted on kerbs at junctions and along the middle of the roads to aid visibility in the blackout. Destination signs on bus stops and shelters were either painted out or removed to confuse the enemy in case of an invasion and all orders for new shelters were cancelled for the duration. Driving conditions were hazardous, especially during the long winter nights, and it was little wonder that there were a number of fatalities, mostly involving pedestrians. The bus crews were paid a wartime bonus.

At the beginning of the war the Corporation was running the following services:

1	Bury Road–Rochdale–Castleton
2	Rochdale-Healey
3	Newhay-Rochdale-Littleborough
4	Rochdale-Wardle
5	Belfield-Rochdale-Bamford
6	Newhay-Rochdale-Summit
8	Littleborough locals
9	Rochdale-Oldham-Ashton
9A	Rochdale-Norden via Spotland Road
9C	Rochdale-Norden via Mellor Street
10	Syke-Rochdale-Turf Hill
12	Railway Station-Rochdale-Spotland
15	Rochdale-Shaw
16	Rochdale-Bacup
17	Rochdale-Manchester via Drake St
17T	Rochdale-Castleton via Tweedale St
19	Rochdale-Bury via Jericho
20	Rochdale-Todmorden
21	Rochdale-Bury via Heywood
23	Rochdale-Bolton

Some months previously the Traffic Commissioner had instructed all bus operators to prepare contingency plans designed to save 50% of the fuel they were then using, while maintaining a full service for workmen. Mr Cherry had produced a scheme for all services to be halved between the peaks and after 6.30pm in the evening; last buses were to run at 9.30pm and Sunday services would not start until after 1pm. The Todmorden express (20) would come off except for one journey in each peak and on Saturday afternoons. The Bury service (21) would be curtailed at Heywood, and the Bolton service (23) would be withdrawn completely.

The revisions were brought in on 25th September 1939. Generally, the cuts were seen as a necessity to be endured, but the withdrawal of Sunday morning services provoked furious protests from the Churches. Eventually, the Transport Department was able to get a supplementary allocation of fuel, which, together with the addition of creosote from the town's gasworks, enabled the improvement of service levels to 65% by November and 75% by March 1940. The contentious Sunday cuts were reinstated in the December.

Two of the older Dennis single-deckers (31 and 32) were converted to mobile hospital units with two more (33 and 34) becoming ambulances and twelve single-deck service buses were equipped with fittings enabling them to carry up to twelve stretchers at a few minutes notice. The basement of the Mellor Street offices was converted into an air raid shelter for the use of the staff.

Before the war, tenders had been invited for 20 more double-deckers to replace the remaining Dennises and petrol-engined Crossleys. Having considered the current condition of the older buses in the fleet, it had been decided to order ten Leyland TD7s, five each with English Electric and Eastern Coach Works bodies and ten Daimler COG6s also with Eastern Coach Works bodies. They arrived in 1940; the Leylands numbered 167-76 (EDK645-54) and the Daimlers 177-86 (EDK686-65). The body of withdrawn Condor 106 was in good condition and was fitted to the chassis of 82, which was then renumbered 106. There were to be no more new buses for another three years, but there would only be 13 buses in the fleet more than eight years old, which was to stand the Corporation in good stead for the long haul ahead.

Circulars from the Ministry of War Transport were coming out thick and fast, one requesting

The 1939 order for 20 buses, split equally between Leyland and Daimler, arrived in 1940.

Left. Number 171, the last of five Leyland Titan TD7s with English Electric 56-seat bodies, stands in South Parade on service 10. *(JHC)*

Below. The second five Leylands carried ECW bodies. Number 172 stands outside the General Post Office. *(STA)*

Right. The ten Daimler COG6s also carried ECW bodies identical to those on the Leylands. Number 182 is pictured in South Parade with a Manchester Leyland PD1 behind. *(JHC)*

operators to grant free transport to members of the armed forces in uniform. The Transport Committee was unhappy with the effect on revenue and instead proposed a penny maximum fare. However, this was obviously an emotive issue and was voted down in Council, and free travel was implemented.

Another circular raised the permissible laden weight of double-deckers from 10½ tons to 11 tons "*in view of the fact that the use of alternative materials due to war conditions was likely to increase the weight of the vehicles*". What the alternative materials might be was not specified. Mr Cherry was granted his long-standing wish with the imposition of staggered working hours in workshops and factories. At the end of the year the Belfield service (5) was rerouted along Reservoir Street to serve the new Clover Hall Estate on Albert Royds Street.

Blackout conditions, fuel rationing, a period of frost and snow which was the worst for many years and the call up of staff into the armed forces combined to present the Transport Department with a host of difficulties at the beginning of 1940. Four buses were adapted to carry angled snowploughs and worked through the night to keep roads open. Owing to the reluctance of people to travel in the blackout there was a serious drop in revenue, but as the evenings grew lighter the buses became more crowded and revenue started to recover. Unfortunately, the price of materials, wages and fuel was also rising rapidly resulting in increased operating costs of some £20,000 a year.

One issue that raised its head at this time was the question of trousers or skirts for women conductors. The 'modern' element wanted to wear trousers, but they were apparently in the minority and, as the uniforms had already been issued, the Transport Committee decided that no changes should be made.

In March 1940 it was decided, somewhat optimistically, to invite tenders for a further 25 double-deckers. Surprisingly, the Regional Traffic Commissioner approved the application and orders were placed for 25 Leyland TD7s, 20 to be bodied by Eastern Coach Works and five by East Lancashire Coachbuilders of Blackburn. Unfortunately, these never materialised as Leyland were fully committed to building tanks. Spare parts were becoming in short supply, so ten Condors and one Alpha were cannibalised to keep the rest of the fleet on the road.

During October 1940 a comprehensive scheme for mutual aid was drawn up between 30 municipal undertakings and four companies in the region and agreement was reached on the pooling of garage accommodation and hiring of buses in the event of any of the operators suffering damage by enemy air raids. At the request of the Regional Traffic Commissioner, Rochdale loaned drivers to Midland Red for work in the Coventry area.

On 20th October 1940 the through service to Bury (21), which had been split at Heywood for over a year, was reinstated. Before the war there had been a ten minute frequency but while Rochdale had maintained a 20 minute service to Heywood, Bury had only been able to run half hourly on their portion of the route. Dissatisfied with this arrangement Bury had applied to the Traffic Commissioners for extra fuel to reinstate the through service every 20 minutes, but this was refused and instead a 30-minute service was operated with additional journeys between Rochdale and Heywood during the peaks.

So far there had been little tangible evidence of the war as Rochdale was on the fringe of the Manchester conurbation, but in January 1941 the first enemy bombs fell on the town when Manchester Road, Sudden was closed for a time and the Manchester, Heywood and Bury services were disrupted.

More Government directives were received. The War Transport (Standing Passengers) Order raised the maximum standing passengers to 30 on single-deck buses "*with alternative seating arrangements*" and most of the single-deckers were converted to standees with perimeter seating during the next two years. The War Transport (Standing Passengers) No 2 Order followed shortly, raising the maximum permitted standing passengers on unmodified single-deckers and in the lower saloons of double-deckers to 12, resulting in the unfortunate conductor having difficulty in collecting fares as well as supervising the platform. The solution, as in some other undertakings, was to employ auxiliary conductors. These were regular travellers who were willing to ride on the platform, ring the bell to stop and start the bus, and announce the name of the stop, but were not responsible for collecting fares. For this they were allowed to travel free on the journey concerned.

In February 1942 Rochdale's General Manager, Mr George Cherry resigned to become General Manager at Birkenhead. Mr Cherry had been at Rochdale for six years and his main legacy was to return a loss-making operation to profitability. His successor at Rochdale was Mr Chaceley T Humpidge, Chief Engineer and Chief Assistant at Nottingham City Transport.

A native of Staffordshire, Mr Humpidge had gained a degree in engineering at Birmingham University. He had started his transport career as an assistant engineer with Birmingham City Transport in 1928. Six years later he was appointed Chief Assistant Engineer at Liverpool and in 1937 Chief Engineer and Assistant Manager at Portsmouth, moving to Nottingham in 1940.

Mr Chaceley T Humpidge wearing his chain of office as President of the Municipal Passenger Transport Association during his later time as manager of the Sheffield undertaking. *(STA)*

THE DARKEST HOUR

The loss of Burma and Malaya to the Japanese in 1942 cut off supplies of rubber and led to a further tightening of belts. The Regional Traffic Commissioner first instructed all operators to bring forward the departure time of last buses from town centres to 10pm, although this did not affect Rochdale as there was already a 9.30pm finish, but later in the year he demanded more drastic reductions to achieve a further 10% saving in mileage, while retaining the full workmen's services.

The scheme produced by Mr Humpidge included last buses leaving no later than 9pm and Sunday services starting after 2pm. Service 12 (Spotland – Railway Station) was cut back to the town centre with Service 21 re-routed along Tweedale Street and Maclure Road to cover, and most of the extra journeys on weekday afternoons were withdrawn. The revisions came into operation on Sunday 27th December 1942.

By now the cuts were really starting to hurt and caused a great deal of controversy. Public and Councillors fully agreed with the need for economies, so long as they were on someone else's route and there were many complaints of overcrowding and passengers being left behind throughout the system. Councillor Sharrocks, the Chairman of the Transport Committee, was at pains to point out that the revisions had still only achieved a 5.8% reduction against the 10% called for, and there could yet be worse to come. Nonetheless, the Sunday cuts once again attracted vociferous opposition, with Rochdale's MP writing to the Minister for War Transport, only to be told that transport facilities in the Rochdale area were considered to be adequate. Despite this an application was made to the Traffic Commissioner for a skeleton service on major routes, but it was flatly rejected.

Sickness among drivers and conductors had risen to more than twice the level before the war, and much of it was attributed to the continual strain of driving in the blackout or trying to collect fares on packed buses in virtual darkness. Coincidentally, an advert in the local paper extolled the virtues of Aspro tablets for, among other things, steadying the nerves of bus drivers during the blackout. There was also a shortage of blue paint so it was decided to paint older buses grey if and when required.

With the continuing shortage of fuel, the Government instructed all larger operators with over 100 vehicles to convert 10% of their fleet to use Producer Gas. The coke-fired gas plant produced fumes which, when mixed with water vapour formed a gas, which could be mixed with diesel fuel in the cylinders, although it reduced the engine's power by about a third and was impractical on hilly routes. The trailer was towed behind the bus, which precluded its use on any route involving a reverse.

Rochdale's target was twelve buses by July 1943 but the work went slowly. The Transport Committee inspected the first bus in mid April but by the planned date only five vehicles had been converted, Leyland TS7 single-decker 3 operating on the Healey route (2) and Condor 119 and Leyland TD5s 162, 163 and 166 on the Bury via Heywood route (21). Because of the low power available the converted buses ran on diesel during the heavily loaded morning peak period and the gas trailer was then attached, only to be removed again for the evening peak. It was intended to use more converted buses on the Littleborough – Newhay service (3) if Beresford Street, Newhay could be surfaced to avoid reversing at Newhay terminus, but in the event this was not done and the experiment was abandoned during 1944.

Two small changes were made to services during 1943. The two weekday journeys on the Todmorden service (20) were withdrawn and, following a string of complaints of poor connections between Rochdale and Oldham services at Thornham, the two services were linked to run through between Rochdale and Hathershaw.

More buses were needed to replace worn out and cannibalised Crossleys. New bus production was now limited to Daimler and Guy and they were supplied under the Acquisition and Disposal of Motor Vehicles Order, 1941, on permits issued by the Regional Traffic Commissioner. Rochdale obtained 13 new buses during 1943 and 1944, a mixture of Daimler CWA6 and CWG5 with Massey, Duple and Northern Counties 56-seat austerity bodies, with fewer opening windows, front indicators only and wooden, slatted seats numbered 187-99 (EDK771, 798-809).

LIGHT AT THE END OF THE TUNNEL

The German retreat on all fronts culminating in the D-Day landings in France in June 1944 reversed the fortunes of the war. The Allies were now winning and a new spirit of optimism was apparent.

With the war in Europe drawing to a close plans were being made for the coming peace. The Council were already developing a scheme for a large new housing estate at Kirkholt, south of Oldham Road and east of Queensway,

During 1943 and 1944 Rochdale took delivery of 13 austerity Daimlers with various makes of body.

Number 187, delivered in 1943 with a Massey 56-seat body, pauses at Middleton on its way from Manchester to Rochdale on service 17. The bus was delivered from the bodybuilders in a non standard livery. *(MMT)*

Number 190, with a very angular body by Duple, stands on the Smith Street bus park in the early fifties. *(JHC)*

Number 191, a further variation with a more rounded Northern Counties body, leaves the Butts on service 10 to Turf Hill. The art-deco Burtons building in the background is now a building society. *(PDC)*

which would accommodate up to 10,000 people displaced by the clearance of many back-to-back houses within walking distance of the town centre. Together with a smaller development at Greave between Edenfield Road and Bury Road, this was obviously going to have a great effect on the provision of bus services in post-war Rochdale.

In April 1944 Mr Humpidge had spoken to the Rochdale Rotary Club about the problems he anticipated after the war. He drew attention to the fact that housing development was taking up more and more land for a similar number of people, and was also further away from the town centre, which meant more mileage and more buses for no more traffic.

In his opinion a procession of 56-seat motorbuses, each with a driver and conductor, was a waste of road space, and considered that obsolete government regulations limiting the size of buses would hold back progress after the war. Mr Humpidge favoured an increase in the maximum permitted length of two-axle buses to 30ft with a width of 8ft.

Plans were drawn up to roof over the existing depot yard and to build new offices on the Mellor Street frontage.

In general, long distance coach services, particularly those aimed at the holiday market, had been suspended during the war. For operators like Yelloway, whose business relied heavily on this type of traffic, the effect had been little short

of a disaster. Faced with a need for finance to keep the business afloat until normal services could be resumed, Yelloway approached Manchester, Oldham and Rochdale Corporations early in 1944 with a view to buying their Rochdale to Manchester express service. After lengthy negotiations the sale was agreed at a price of £38,500, Rochdale's share of the cost being £8,106.

Rochdale was allocated one all-day working on the route. The service, which had previously operated out of Yelloway's Weir Street bus station, was found a stand nearby in Smith Street and was given the number 24, which was not used by either Rochdale or Oldham, but caused Manchester to renumber its Cheetham Hill to Moston route from 24 to 26.

With the service came two buses, an all-Leyland TD5 dating from 1938 which became 130 (DDK257) and a Beadle coach-bodied AEC Regal (JD1381) new to the London Co-operative Society in 1931, which never received a fleet number and was only used on private hire work. There was another Regal (DK7396), new to Yelloway in 1931, which apparently never ran in service and was withdrawn by 1950. A second double-decker, a Duple austerity-bodied Daimler CWG5 was currently on order by Yelloway, and Rochdale successfully applied to the Regional Traffic Commissioner for it to be diverted to them, becoming 200 (EDK835). The service was taken over on 18th June 1944.

Daimler CWG5 number 200 is on the left of this trio standing on the bus park. *(JHC)*

In September 1944, with the end of enemy air raids, blackout restrictions were eased on the main roads and in the town centre and in November the Regional Traffic Commissioner relaxed the curfew and allowed last buses to leave the town centre at 10pm, instead of 9pm as they had done for over two years. Revised schedules were drawn up, but were rejected by the platform staff on the grounds that the new late duties meant being away from home for up to twelve hours, which was particularly onerous for the conductresses who were mostly married women and still had a home to run.

Negotiations dragged on, compromises were made and the new schedules came into operation in time for Christmas. However, despite representations from the churches and the local Member of Parliament, the Regional Traffic Commissioner steadfastly refused permission for the restoration of Sunday morning services and they were not reinstated until after the end of hostilities.

Things were starting to move. Application was made to the Regional Traffic Commissioner for an allocation of ten new buses, a plot of land on the north side of Smith Street was leased for a bus park and it was decided to mark the impending victory with an illuminated bus.

On 9th May 1945 the war ended in Europe. Overnight, the masks over the headlights and saloon lighting were removed, the white patches on the mudguards and rear corners were quickly painted out and a semblance of normality returned..

CO-ORDINATION AND NATIONALISATION

The euphoria at the coming of peace did not last long. The war was still going on in the Far East and there were shortages and rationing at home, so things did not change very much in practical terms for the average Rochdale resident. There was a need to concentrate scarce resources on rebuilding the damaged or worn out infrastructure, there were arrears of maintenance and a shortage of spare parts and many of the Departments employees were still away in the armed forces. Perversely, after years of restrictions demand for travel was booming.

Co-ordination was again in the air and on 20th June 1945 the Municipal Passenger Transport

This withdrawn Crossley Alpha, number 63, had been decorated to celebrate the end of the war. *(MMT)*

Association convened a conference in Manchester, attended by representatives from all the municipal transport operators in the area, to consider how best to secure this in the planning of post war passenger services, particularly in regard to future satellite towns, new housing estates and new industries. A Joint Transport Advisory Committee was set up consisting of representatives of Ashton-under-Lyne, Bolton, Bury, Manchester, Oldham, Rochdale, Salford and Stockport Corporations and the SHMD Board.

At the General Election on 5th July 1945, a Labour government, committed to the nationalisation of all means of production and distribution, was elected with a large majority. This sent shock waves throughout the transport industry, although municipal undertakings, being already in public ownership, did not at first foresee a problem, wrongly assuming that nationalisation would only apply to private companies. However, as details of the draft Transport Bill came out, it became clear that its scope was to be far wider reaching than anticipated.

The Bill proposed the establishment of a British Transport Commission to provide an adequate, economical and integrated system of transport, and included the transfer of all undertakings operating passenger transport services to a number of Area Transport Boards. While Rochdale, like the other municipalities in the area, had been happy to consider voluntary co-ordination of certain conditions, there was no way they were willingly going to give up control of their undertaking. Their philosophy was that public services should be "run by local people for the benefit of local people."

So, a letter was sent to local Members of Parliament setting out the Corporations views, which were that it was already running an efficient and economical undertaking, that the Traffic Commissioner could ensure that there was proper co-ordination and that local control was more likely to respond to local needs than a regional or national authority.

But, while opinion in the Council was largely divided along party lines, there was one huge area of contention on which everyone was united. This was the small amount of compensation that the Government proposed to pay, which in Rochdale's case was a mere £10,000. As one councillor put it, the government had reached a rather remarkable compromise between compensation and confiscation by paying compensation that was so tiny that it was confiscation spoken rather softly. In his view, the government, in its zeal for nationalisation, was treating Municipal Corporations as full-blown capitalists, and they were penalising the working classes whose money had put those undertaking in a sound financial position.

Another councillor considered that the government wanted the goods for next to nothing so they could make a profit and thereby prove nationalisation a success. It was pointed out that the whole Transport Department would be taken over for the price of four new buses. Adversity makes strange bedfellows and the Corporation found unlikely allies in the trades unions who were concerned that employees would lose touch with local management if they were all submerged in a national organisation.

Opinion among the municipalities was divided, those in deficit generally being for and those in profit against. The Government was not swayed by the arguments and the Bill subsequently became the Road Traffic Act, 1947, becoming law on 1st January 1948.

Not long after, in a talk to the Rochdale Rotary Club, Mr Humpidge observed that something had needed to be done if the cut-throat competition between road and rail was not to be resumed after the war, but the Transport Act had been hastily conceived and inadequately discussed, and mistakes had been made which would have to be put right later. He remained convinced that co-ordination of road and rail was essential, but his main fear was that once transport was nationalised there would be no competition and, therefore, no guarantee of efficiency, economy or enterprise.

Despite the passing of the Act, the South East Lancashire and East Cheshire Municipal Passenger Transport Association Joint Advisory Committee, an indigestible title if ever there was one, continued to meet regularly in an attempt to standardise conditions of workmen's and children's fares, carriage of dogs and parcels, half fare computations and the like, but could never get agreement between the constituent operators and, in the face of more pressing matters, interest declined until eventually the committee was disbanded.

Although nationalisation of the private bus companies happened fairly quickly, the draft proposals for a Northern Area Transport Board were not published until October 1949. Shortly afterwards, on 23rd February 1950, a further General Election resulted in the government being returned with an unworkably small majority. Faced with mounting unpopularity in a population that had endured a period of austerity and rationing as long as the war itself, the government again went to the country and on 25th October 1951 they were swept from power. While nationalisation remained, the scheme for area boards was quietly dropped, not to be resurrected until the plans for Conurbation Transport Executives some 15 years later.

STARTING AGAIN

Away from the national scene there was still a need to get on with running the job at a local level. The proposal for a central bus station again reared its head. Since the 1933 debacle the subject had not been mentioned again, but now it was proposed to build a new bus station on land bordered by Smith Street, River Street, Water Street and the River Roch. The scheme was approved in principle and was included in the draft Town Plan. The Ministry of Transport gave its approval, a compulsory purchase order was obtained and work commenced on the detailed planning.

However, there was no money yet for schemes of this nature and once again nothing came of the proposal. Although meetings were held sporadically the scheme was officially laid to rest in March 1951, but ironically the new bus station currently planned more than fifty years later will occupy exactly the same site.

The Regional Traffic Commissioner issued the necessary licence for the ten new buses, all of which were to be Daimlers, four CWD6s with the new Daimler CD6 engine, and six CWA6s with AEC engines, bodied by Massey to the 'relaxed austerity' specification with improved seating, more opening windows and the Manchester-style indicator layout. They were delivered towards the end of the year as 21-30 (EDK921-30). At the same time 13 existing austerity-bodied Daimlers were modified with Manchester indicators while

Rochdale's first post-war buses were ten Daimlers fitted with Massey 'relaxed austerity' bodies, with improved seating and ventilation and Manchester-style indicators delivered in November 1945. The last of these, number 30, stands in South Parade. *(JHC)*

BUS OVERTURNS AT FIELDHOUSE

PASSENGERS ESCAPE THROUGH WINDOWS

In the upper picture Cravens-bodied Leyland Titan TD5c 143 lies on its side on Cronkeyshaw Common after overturning when the driver swerved to avoid a child. *(RO)*

The body was written off and the chassis was dispatched to Wigan and gained a new Massey body with a central entrance and sliding doors. Number 143 is pictured *(lower)* on the Town Hall Square on its return. *(RLS)*

Five AEC Regent IIIs with Weymann bodies were ordered in 1945, although they did not arrive until two years later. Here number 34 turns across the Esplanade with the Town Hall in the background. *(JHC)*

conventional gearboxes replaced the torque converters on the seven Leyland TD5cs 128-9 and 140-4.

Sunday morning services were finally reinstated on 29th July 1945, and during the year the use of auxiliary conductors came to an end, creosote fuel was discontinued and the temporary standing arrangements ceased. Things were starting to return to normal.

Late in 1945 the Regional Traffic Commissioner authorised five more buses. These were AEC Regent IIIs with Weymann bodies numbered 31-5 (FDK331-5), but due to the heavy demand for new buses there was a lengthy waiting list and they were not delivered until 1947.

At the same time Mr Humpidge had been looking at fitting buses with platform doors and the Passenger Transport Committee had authorised one as an experiment. The opportunity came on 1st December when 143, a 1938 Cravens-bodied Leyland TD5, was involved in an accident on Binns Nook Road while working the Syke service, overturning when the driver swerved to avoid a child. The body was damaged beyond repair and a new Massey body was ordered as a replacement,

incorporating a central entrance with a sliding door.

The bus returned to service in December 1946 working a regular duty on the Rochdale to Bury route (19), but although it was said to be operating satisfactorily, 143 remained the only one of its kind and was the first of the batch to be withdrawn in 1951.

The issue of licences by the Ministry of Transport for the purchase and disposal of vehicles ceased from 1st January 1946 and an order was quickly placed for a further twenty buses to replace all the remaining Crossleys including the two 1935 Mancunians. These were to be AEC Regent IIIs, thirteen with Weymann bodies identical to the previous batch and the last seven bodied by East Lancashire Coachbuilders of Blackburn. Initially, they were all to be 7ft 6in wide, but when the maximum permitted width was increased to 8ft an attempt was made to change the order accordingly. Weymann could not oblige but East Lancs could, and the buses were delivered in 1948, the former numbered 36-48 (GDK136-48) and the latter starting a new block as 201-7 (GDK401-7).

The 1946 order was for another 20 Regent IIIs. The first 13 had Weymann bodies identical to the 31-35 batch. Number 42 is shown above crossing the town centre in the 1950s. *(MMT)*

The last seven carried East Lancs bodies and were built to the newly approved 8ft width. Below, number 206 stands outside Yates's Wine Lodge in Newgate having arrived from Norden via Spotland Road, the indicators already changed ready for it to run round to South Parade for its return journey via Mellor Street. *(PDC)*

Routes had to be cleared for 8ft wide operation and the list eventually authorised by the Traffic Commissioner comprised Littleborough, Summit and Todmorden (3/6/20), Newhay (3/6), Oldham and Ashton (9), Norden (9A/C), Bacup (16), Bury via Heywood (21), Manchester via Castleton (17) and Manchester via Chadderton (24). On the latter, however, the Chief Constable refused to allow the wider buses to run along Wood Street, so the service was diverted along Drake Street. All other routes were to remain at the old limit until the restriction was removed completely in 1950.

In early 1947 a further fifteen Weymann-bodied Regent IIIs were ordered, bringing the total of new buses on order up to forty. These were not delivered until 1949 and were numbered 208-22 (GDK708-22). The buses that were to be replaced were in poor condition and some had to be withdrawn ahead of their replacements being delivered; so six buses were hired from Bury

Corporation to bridge the gap. In view of the economic conditions in the country the Ministry of Transport wrote to the Corporation asking them to reduce the current orders, but the Council would not agree.

In 1948 Mr Humpidge acquired six second-hand AEC Regents:

71 BWA212 Weymann 1935
72 CWA492 Weymann 1936
from Sheffield,
73 JX6425 Park Royal 1938
74 JX6568 Roe 1938
75 JX6569 Roe 1938
76 JX6570 Roe 1938
from Halifax.

The Sheffield buses were fitted with the Manchester-style front indicator display but the Halifax ones retained their originals and all were painted in Rochdale blue and cream before entering service.

Fifteen more Regent IIIs were ordered in 1947. These carried the 8ft wide version of the standard Weymann body and were numbered 208-22. On a wet winter day 214, in the later cream livery, climbs up Smithy Bridge Road on its way from Hollingworth Lake to Rochdale on one of the numerous variants of service 8. *(PDC)*

During 1948 six second-hand Regents were bought from Sheffield and Halifax due to the prolonged delivery time for new buses. In the picture above number 71, a Weymann-bodied Regent new to Sheffield Joint Omnibus Committee in 1935, stands on the bus park after repainting and fitting with Manchester style destination indicators. *(PDC)*

The lower picture shows former Halifax Corporation Park Royal-bodied Regent number 73, new in 1938, outside the General Post Office. *(PDC)*

ROCHDALE CORPORATION TRANSPORT SERVICE

The Rochdale Corporation provides omnibus services in the county borough, and also the surrounding districts, i.e., the urban districts of LITTLEBOROUGH, MILNROW, SHAW, WARDLE and WHITWORTH.

The Corporation also provides through services to the following towns:—ASHTON, BACUP, BURY, HEYWOOD, MANCHESTER, OLDHAM, TODMORDEN. Special 'buses may also be hired for Special events, outings, etc., within a limited radius of Rochdale Town Centre. The Corporation also operates a parcels and light goods collection and delivery service in Rochdale, and district; also to MANCHESTER, BURY, and OLDHAM. Parcels may be collected from home or handed in at the Centre Inquiry Office and Parcels Offices at the Butts. There are also left luggage facilities at the Butts Office.

For all inquiries and complaints please write to
THE GENERAL MANAGER
CORPORATION TRANSPORT OFFICE
MELLOR STREET, ROCHDALE, LANCS.

A page from the 1949 Rochdale Council handbook. Although there were newer buses in the fleet, the designer used this picture of ten-year-old number 143, because its central entrance and sliding doors portrayed the much more modern image he wanted to project. *(RLS)*

A further ten Weymann-bodied AEC Regent IIIs were ordered in 1948 to what was by now becoming a standard design. These were to be numbered 223-32 (HDK23-32) and were delivered in 1950.

Meanwhile, still desperate for serviceable buses and also short of manpower in the workshops, arrangements were made for twenty vehicles to have their bodies refurbished by Samlesbury Engineering Ltd of Blackburn. However, some of these buses were found to be too far-gone to be patched up, and eventually seven received new Samlesbury 7ft 9in wide bodies. These were 1935-1937 AEC Regents 120-125 and 137, which were not returned to service until 1951, but lasted for a further six years.

More new buses were ordered during 1949. The five Cravens-bodied Leyland Tigers working the Castleton route (1) dated from 1937. After working hard through the war they were beginning to show their age and would be due for replacement in a couple of years. At the same time AEC had released details of what was then a revolutionary under floor-engined chassis to be known as the Regal IV and invited expressions

of interest. Rochdale placed a tentative order for five, later increasing it to a firm order for seven. The two-door bodies were by East Lancs to the newly authorised 30ft length and seated 42, an increase of seven over the Tigers they were to replace. They arrived towards the end of 1951 numbered 301-7 (HDK701-7).

The rest of the order was for a further five of the tried and tested Regent III, although this time they carried East Lancs 5-bay bodies. Delivered early in 1952 they were numbered 233-7 (HDK833-7) and were the last exposed-radiator buses in the fleet.

A great deal of work also needed to be done on the Mellor Street depot and workshops, which had remained substantially unchanged since the final tramway conversions in 1932 and no more than the minimum maintenance had been done on the buildings during the war. It was proposed to roof over the depot yard on the east side of Mellor Street and the open land next to the workshops across the road and in December 1947 tenders were also invited for the construction of inspection and repair pits, extensions and alterations to the workshops and replacement of the works roof,

Number 225, one of the last batch of Weymann-bodied Regents ordered in 1948, waits on the Littleborough stand outside the Regal Cinema. The cinema is now a pub and restaurant called the Regal Moon. *(MMT)*

On a typically wet and windy Rochdale day, the second of the next generation single-deckers, under-floor engined AEC Regal IV number 302, by now renumbered 2, stands in the Butts waiting time before pulling onto its departure stand. Behind the bus can be seen the Corporation's town centre offices which replaced those on the tramway centre in 1935 and remained in use until the new bus station opened in 1978. *(MMT)*

Number 304 of the same batch looks more modern pictured here on the bus park in the later cream livery. *(MMT)*

and alterations to the entrances and provision of new aluminium shutter gates. However, the work was shelved due to the shortage of materials and it was not until 1950 that it was possible to start work on the scheme.

THE GROWING NETWORK

Although the continuing shortage of buses and crews was generally, at least in the beginning, the result of difficulty in maintaining the fleet during the war, there were two other contributory factors; the increase in demand for travel and the construction of new housing estates on the outskirts of the town.

To cater for changes in traffic flows resulting from the new 160-home Greave estate on Sandy Lane, services in the Bamford area were reorganised on 2nd March 1947. The Castleton to Bury Road service (1) was curtailed to operate between Rochdale and Castleton only, The Rochdale to Wardle service (4) was extended across Rochdale to Greave via Bury Road and Sandy Lane and renumbered 7, The Belfield to Bamford service via Sandy Lane was split in the town centre as Rochdale to Bamford via Bury Road (5) with the Rochdale to Belfield section becoming 14 and a new service was introduced between Rochdale and Bamford via Mellor Street and Edenfield Road (4).

At the same time Manchester's service 4 was extended from Bamford (Burns Tavern) to the junction of Edenfield Road and Bagslate Moor Road. This resulted in two number 4 services running along Bagslate Moor Road, one to Rochdale and one to Manchester, a confusing situation which was slightly alleviated later when Rochdale's 4 was rerouted off Mellor Street and along Spotland Road, thereby becoming 4A.

Following representations from Littleborough District Council, the pre-war frequencies on the Littleborough local service (8) were reinstated and through journeys commenced between Rochdale and Hollingworth Lake, also numbered 8. On 17th October 1948 a couple of journeys between Littleborough and Calderbrook were diverted to serve High Peak, Rochdale's name for the small hamlet of Lidgate, nestling under Blackstone Edge, where a service had been requested, and

refused, some 20 years previously. At the same time Littleborough asked for the re-instatement of the weekday services on the Rochdale-Todmorden service (20), but while Rochdale were willing, Todmorden were not and there was to be no regular daily service across Summit, other than the Ribble X4, until PTE days.

On 18th October 1948 the Norden service (9A/9C), was renumbered 11A/11C, which, with the demise of the Blackstone Edge route many years before, had remained vacant. 9B was still used for the rush hour Bagslate-Broad Lane journeys, later to be cut back to operate between Rochdale and Broad Lane only.

The first houses on the sprawling new council estate at Kirkholt were occupied at the end of 1948 and a new service (18) was introduced from the town centre along Oldham Road, Queensway and Daventry Road, commencing on 3rd January 1949.

During 1948 requests were received for limited stop journeys on the two routes to Manchester via Castleton (17) and Royton (24). Manchester, Rochdale and Oldham proposed to divert service 24 via Chadderton Town Hall putting an extra four minutes on the running time, and introducing a peak hour express service (90) observing service 24 stops between Rochdale and Royton, then non-stop to Manchester (Stevenson Square). The express service over the 17 route observed main stopping places between Rochdale and Middleton then non-stop to Manchester (Cannon Street). As an example of Rochdale's haphazard and often confusing service numbering policy the express journeys also showed 17, although under pressure from Manchester they were renumbered to yet another service 8 from 19th February 1951!

The revisions to service 24 came into operation on Sunday 1st May 1949 with the express services starting the following morning, the delay being due to protracted negotiations on the interavailability of return tickets between service 90 and the parallel Manchester, Oldham and North Western Road Car service 2 between Royton and Manchester. At the same time the last departures on services from the town centre were restored to their pre-war time of 11pm.

There had also been requests for a peripheral service from Castleton to Halifax Road via Queensway, Kingsway and Albert Royds Street, mainly for the benefit of workers at the Castleton mills. However, Mr Humpidge was not in favour of a service with such limited potential and instead produced his own scheme to extend the Belfield service (14) along Kingsway as far as Oldham Road.

Services were again re-organised with the Wardle route (7) curtailed in the town centre and Greave linked to Kingsway as new route 14. These changes also came in on 1st May 1949.

On 9th July 1949 the Rochdale-Birch Hill journeys (3B) were extended into the grounds of Birch Hill Hospital. This prompted Littleborough District Council to ask for a similar facility from Littleborough, which was refused.

When all these changes had been made the network assumed the shape that, with a few minor amendments, was to last for the next twenty years. The list of services was:

1	Rochdale-Castleton via Deeplish
2	Rochdale-Healey
3	Newhay-Rochdale-Littleborough via Entwisle Road
3A	Newhay-Rochdale-Littleborough via John Street
3B	Rochdale-Birch Hill
4	Bagslate-Manchester (by MCT)
4	Rochdale-Bamford via Mellor Street
5	Rochdale-Bamford via Bury Road
6	Newhay–Rochdale-Littleborough Summit via Entwisle Road
6A	Newhay-Rochdale-Littleborough Summit via John Street
7	Rochdale-Wardle via Entwisle Road
7A	Rochdale-Wardle via John Street
8	Littleborough Local Services
8	Rochdale-Hollingworth Lake
8	Rochdale-Manchester express
9	Rochdale-Ashton
9B	Bagslate-Rochdale-Broad Lane
10	Syke-Rochdale-Turf Hill
11A	Rochdale-Norden via Spotland Road
11C	Rochdale-Norden via Mellor Street
12A	Rochdale-Daniel Fold or Lanehead
14	Kingsway-Rochdale-Greave
15	Rochdale-Shaw
16	Rochdale-Bacup
17	Rochdale-Manchester
17T	Rochdale-Castleton via Tweedale St
18	Rochdale-Kirkholt
19	Rochdale-Bury via Jericho
20	Rochdale-Todmorden
21T	Rochdale-Bury via Heywood
24	Rochdale-Royton-Manchester
90	Rochdale-Royton-Manchester express

In November 1949 the residents of the small Chesham housing estate on the Middleton boundary asked for the Rochdale-Chesham Avenue short workings (17T) to be extended along Chesham Avenue into the estate. However, the road needed strengthening and widening and the trees cutting back, which the Highways Committee were unwilling to do. So the Transport Committee were able to note, with deep regret, the decision of the Highways Committee which had prevented them from improving the bus service for the benefit of the public on the estate. Several other attempts were made over the years to obtain a service but with no success and nowadays neither the 17T nor its successor, the 443, exists.

NOTHING NEW

Trouble on the buses is not just a present day phenomenon. In June 1949 a 17 year-old youth appeared at Rochdale Magistrates Court on a charge of assaulting a bus conductor on Halifax Road. He had tendered half a crown for three 2d fares and had received his two shillings change all in copper coins. An argument followed and the conductor had received a black eye. The defendant was bound over to keep the peace for twelve months and ordered to pay twelve shillings costs, the Magistrate commenting that he must learn not to throw his weight around just because he was a big lad and the conductor was small.

Graffiti on buses is nothing new either. On the evening of 22nd October 1950, while the driver and conductor of a Corporation bus waited at Daniel Fold, four boys daubed the rear of the bus with black paint in the form of a circle enclosing a cross. On appearing at the Rochdale Juvenile Court the Chairman tried to discover the subject of the mystic symbol, but none of the offenders offered any explanation, although they all denied that it represented anything to do with either the Black Hand gang or death to all conductors. The boys, aged between eleven and fifteen, were each fined twenty shillings with payment of five shillings costs.

Fruits of Experience

With fifty years experience of public transport operation to support their judgment, Rochdale Corporation have chosen M.C.W. coachwork for their new 'buses. Over eighty bodies, all of the metal construction patented by M.C.W., are included in the fleet of modern vehicles in service or on order. The photograph shows a 59-seater, one of the latest batch to be delivered to Rochdale.

METROPOLITAN - CAMMELL - WEYMANN MOTOR BODIES LTD

VICKERS HOUSE, BROADWAY, WESTMINSTER, LONDON, S.W.I

THE FRUGAL FIFTIES

The decade of the fifties signalled the beginning a long period of falling patronage and rising costs. It started with bus operators at a low point with their fleets still run down from the war and a lengthy wait for new bus orders to be delivered. There was still rationing and Government control of just about everything they needed to rebuild their business and it is interesting to speculate what might have been if the industry had been able to respond quickly and adequately to the immediate post-war desire for travel. However ,by the time new buses started coming into service the boom was over and competition from television and the private car was already making inroads into passenger levels.

In a labour intensive industry such as bus operation costs soared out of proportion to those in manufacturing, so the only policy was to raise fares, and regular above-inflation fares increases during the 1950s only worsened comparisons with the car. However, civic pride rejected advertising on bus sides that could have brought in some extra revenue.

In February 1951 Mr Humpidge, Rochdale's Engineer and General Manager since 1942, moved to Bradford in a similar position. His replacement was Mr Joseph C Franklin, currently Chief Engineer at Salford City Transport. Joe Franklin was 42 years of age and was born in Manchester, although he had family connections with Rochdale. Educated at Manchester's Central High School, he had served his apprenticeship with Crossley Motors before working for Gardeners at Patricroft. In 1937 he was appointed Works Superintendent with the Birmingham and Midland Motor Omnibus Company (Midland Red) becoming Rolling Stock Engineer with Walsall Corporation in 1945. He had been at Salford since 1946.

Mr Franklin took up his post at Rochdale on 1st May 1951 and at the same time the position of Traffic Manager was re-designated Deputy General Manager. Robert Farrar, who had been in charge of running Rochdale's buses ever since their introduction in 1926, was the first holder of the title.

One of Mr Franklin's first actions was to create a five-year programme for new buses and

The last batch of AEC Regent IIIs comprised five with East Lancs 5-bay bodies. Number 233, the first of these, stands in the Butts while working a peak hour 17T journey to Castleton. *(MMT)*

Mr Joe Franklin *(courtesy Eric Ogden)*

withdrawals and initially he placed an order for 38 vehicles. These were 30 Daimler CVG6 with Weymann bodies and the new Birmingham-designed 'tin front', and eight more AEC Regal IV, this time with bodies by HV Burlingham of Blackpool. The first 15 Daimlers numbered 238-52 (JDK738-52) and AECs 308-15 (JDK708-15) arrived in 1953, the remaining 15 Daimlers following early in 1954 numbered 253-67 (KDK653-67).

Mr Franklin also instituted a revue and re-organisation of workshop procedures with a view to increasing efficiency and making economies. One of these was the purchase of an automatic bus washer that cut the time required to wash a bus exterior from an hour to five minutes with a corresponding reduction in garage staff.

The chassis of 185, a Weymann-bodied Daimler COG6 dating from 1940, was in poor condition so, in February 1952, its body was exchanged with the Northern Counties austerity body from Daimler CWG5 198 and was sold for scrap, 198 then being renumbered 185.

The general gloom was gradually lifting and the Coronation of the young Queen Elizabeth II on 2nd June 1953 heralded a period of optimism, the new Elizabethan age. To celebrate the occasion the Mellor Street and town centre premises were suitably decorated and floral displays were placed on top of the bus shelters in the town centre. Pensioners were given free travel on Corporation buses within the Rochdale operating area on Coronation Day.

In September 1953 Mr Farrar retired from his position as Deputy General Manager and Mr Ronald Cox, Traffic Superintendent of Salford City Transport and a former colleague of Mr Franklin took his place. Mr Cox was 37 and had been born in St Helens and started his career there as a junior clerk in the Transport Department in 1935. After war service with RAF Transport Command he returned to St Helens in 1946 as Traffic Officer and two years later moved to Salford. In June 1954 Mr Franklin moved to Blackpool and Mr Cox took over as General Manager.

FINE TUNING

By now the route network had virtually reached its maximum extent and all that remained was a little fine-tuning.

There had been growing concern about overcrowding at peak periods on Ribble's service 244 to Edenfield and Blackburn, and Rochdale Corporation had asked the company on several occasions for extra peak period journeys for workers in the mills at Ashworth and Red Lumb, beyond Norden. These were within the Borough, but since 1924 when Ribble first ran into Rochdale the operating boundary had generally been considered to be the former tram terminus at Mill Bridge. The company were naturally unwilling to send a bus all the way from Blackburn for the mile or so involved and instead, in January 1950, converted the service to double-deck operation.

In the February Rochdale introduced journeys between the town centre and Hollingworth Lake on Saturdays, Sundays and Bank Holidays, but still refused to consider weekday operation outside the peaks.

Fifteen double-deckers, ordered in 1951, were delivered in 1953. These were Daimler CVG6s with a Weymann 59-seat bodies and the Birmingham-style tin front. Number 240 stands in Manchester's Cannon Street bus station when new, about to return to Rochdale on service 17. These were the first buses on which the blue was carried round the front of the lower deck, a variation applied to all buses from then on.

Also new in 1953 were a further seven Regal IVs, this time with bodies by Burlingham of Blackpool, which would replace the last of the pre-war single-deckers. A spotless number 308 stands at the service 1 barrier on the Esplanade opposite the Town Hall. *(both MMT)*

Oldham Corporation wanted to abandon the Chadderton loop on service 24 and Rochdale and Manchester, not being directly concerned, backed their application. The proposal produced a predictable reaction from Chadderton Council and residents, and the Traffic Commissioner refused the application.

Towards the end of 1952 Whitworth Council asked for a service to the new Wallbank estate situated some distance from the main Bacup bus route. However, the roads were unsuitable and Rochdale refused to operate there until they were improved. Eventually, the work was done but the service was not to start until 7th November 1955.

Both Bacup and Littleborough Councils had been less than pleased when the Traffic Commissioners had dismembered the Manchester express network some twenty years earlier and still nurtured hopes of regaining through services to Manchester. Rochdale saw no merit in a service from Bacup and rejected the idea. However, they did see a limited market for one from Littleborough, so to test the water a minimal peak hour service commenced on 17th August 1953 utilising existing Rochdale workings to Littleborough and on the express service (8) to Manchester, one side effect being that yet another service 8 appeared in the Littleborough area. This was not to last for long as there was very little traffic across Rochdale, passengers from Littleborough to Manchester preferring to use the train, and the journeys were withdrawn in late 1954.

In later years Rossendale Transport was to run a short-lived X46 Citysmart express service between Bacup, Rochdale and Manchester, although by a different route between Rochdale and Middleton, while First Manchester also run a couple of peak hour journeys via Rochdale and Royton. But in 1954 this was a long way off and Bacup Council turned its attention to the provision of a local service for the Mettle Cote estates. Rochdale was more amenable to this and agreed to run a service as soon as the roads were made suitable.

However, running time was tight, and had been ever since the conversion from trams, but modern AECs and Daimlers had more power under the bonnet than the old Crossley Condors and eventually, after lengthy negotiations with the trade union, it was agreed to divert one bus an hour via the estates, but only on the journeys towards Rochdale! At least this was up the hill out of Bacup when home-going passengers were loaded with shopping. These journeys commenced on 8th July 1957 but it was a nonsensical situation that could not last long and eventually, nearly a year later on 9th June 1958, hourly journeys towards Bacup were also diverted.

In January 1955 service 15 was extended from Shaw railway station up Grains Road to new housing at Bank House. In the September some peak period Heywood short workings on the Bury service (21T) were re-routed via Manchester Road as 21A.

At the beginning of 1956 a petition was received from residents of the new extension of the Cloverhall estate on the section of Albert Royds Street that was not served by buses, for alternate journeys on service 14 to be diverted via Halifax Road and Albert Royds Street. This was at first refused but when the request was repeated later in the year it was agreed to operate a couple of peak hour journeys for a three-month trial period. However, Mr Cox was not keen to commit extra resources for what he considered would be a waste of time and instead proposed to divert some

Mr Ronald Cox *(courtesy Eric Ogden)*

of the Brocklebank Road short workings along the unserved section of Albert Royds Street to its junction with Halifax Road.

The trial commenced on 7th August 1958 but it didn't take long to confirm that demand was negligible, and the journeys quickly reverted to Brocklebank Road.

More celebrations were in order in 1956 when Rochdale marked the centenary of its inauguration as a Borough. This time, as well as decorating buildings and bus shelters, austerity Daimler 185, the former 198, was illuminated at a cost of £900 and toured the Borough for four weeks in October/November, following which the electrical equipment was stripped out for re-use and the bus was sold for scrap.

With the building of Littleborough Council's new housing estate at Stansfield Farm, some Calderbrook journeys on service 8 were diverted into the estate from 27th May 1957. Then, in March 1958, Milnrow District Council requested a service for their new Holt Estate, built on the hillside above the town. At that time the estate

was outside the Borough boundary and, not for the first time, the Transport Committee turned down such a request. Milnrow, however, did not take no for an answer and sent a delegation to plead their case, the eventual outcome being the extension of certain peak period Kiln Lane short workings into the estate, with a 40-minute frequency on Saturday afternoons. The service commenced on 16th November 1959.

At the same time Whitworth Council asked for the Healey service (2) to be extended to Wallbank for the benefit of Whitworth people working in the factories at Shawclough. When a survey showed that passengers changing buses at Healey Corner were virtually non-existent, the idea was dropped, although many years later the Healey and Wallbank services were to be combined, but purely as an economy measure. The final change of the decade was the extension of the Broad Lane turn-backs on service 9A along Balderstone Road and Hill Top Drive to Friars Crescent to serve the top end of the expanding Kirkholt estate. The new service commenced on 19th October 1959.

In 1955 the Northern Counties Austerity body of Daimler CWA6 199 was rebuilt in the Mellor Street workshops. Despite receiving what amounted to an almost completely new body, the vehicle only lasted another three years before being withdrawn and sold for scrap. *(PDC)*

MORE NEW BUSES

When Mr Cox became General Manager in June 1954 he quickly placed an order for ten AEC Regent Vs with Gardener 6LW engines and Weymann bodies identical to those on the 30 Daimlers. This design of body was to become standard for all future front-engined buses and eventually ran to 85 in all.

The order was quickly extended by a further 30 examples, the last ten having Monocontrol semi-automatic gearboxes instead of the more normal pre-selectors. The buses were numbered 268-97 (NDK968-97) and 298-307 (ODK698-707) and were all delivered in 1956. This saw the demise of the remaining pre-war buses, with the exception of the seven that had been rebodied by Samlesbury in 1951.

At that time Rochdale owned 15 single-deckers, all AEC Regal IVs and none more than four years old, but Mr Cox wanted as far as possible to standardise on an all double-deck fleet and set up a revue of the routes they served.

Service 2 to Healey had been a single-deck route ever since its inception in 1926, but double-deckers had been used on peak hour workings as far as the Healey Hotel at Shawclough for a number of years. The remainder of the route only needed some tree lopping to make it suitable, so at the end of 1956 double-deckers took over the whole operation and early in 1957 three surplus single-deckers, 313-315, were sold to Lancaster Corporation for £6,100.

Meanwhile, another 10 Regent Vs had been ordered, although this time with AEC 9.6 litre engines in place of the Gardner 6LW and the money from the sale of the single-deckers was used to extend the order to eleven. They arrived in

Brand new AEC Regent V number 269, the second of 55 similar buses to be delivered over the next three years, stands outside the AEC factory at Southall in May 1956. Apart from minor differences to fit them to the AEC chassis, the bodies were identical to the 30 Daimlers that had come before. *(STA)*

1957 as 308-18 (RDK408-18) and a further Regal, 311, was sold to Lancaster for £2,000.

With the resulting withdrawal of the seven Samlesbury rebodied examples, pre-war buses were now extinct.

When fleet numbers topped 300 in 1956 the remaining single-deckers were re-numbered to 1-10/12 and at the same time were converted to a single front entrance/exit layout at a cost of £60 per bus to improve safety and increase the seating capacity to 42. Conveniently, it would also make them suitable for one-man operation, although this was not on the agenda at the time.

The revue of single-deck routes had showed only two that were considered unsuitable for double-deck operation. One was service 8 between Littleborough and Calderbrook or Stansfield due to the steep and narrow nature of Calderbrook Road, but this only involved one bus. More important, but more difficult was service 1 to Castleton via Deeplish, Rochdale's first bus route dating from 1926. Here the problem was the low railway bridge over Milkstone Road adjacent to

Rochdale Station and some peak period journeys had already been re-routed along Oldham Road some years earlier so that double-deck vehicles could be used if necessary. Various options were considered to find a solution.

The first was to reroute the service via Richard Street and Miall Street. Lowering the road under Richard Street railway bridge, which was higher, was considered a less expensive option, but the proposed route would have taken the bus service away from the main entrance to the railway station, which was not thought to be a good idea. Attention then turned to the use of low height double-deckers and an AEC Bridgemaster demonstrator 76MME was borrowed for two weeks at the beginning of February 1958. However, Milkstone Road would still have needed lowering by nine inches under the bridge at a prohibitive cost, so in the end nothing was done.

Four more Regent Vs were ordered, this time with platform doors, becoming 319-22 (TDK319-22). 319 was exhibited at the 1958 Commercial Motor Show and entered service in November

The eleven Regent Vs delivered in 1957 signalled a change in policy by having AEC 9.6 litre engines instead of the Gardner CVG6 model as well as Monocontrol semi-automatic transmission. Number 317 is pictured when new outside the Midland Bank while working on service 9. Regent III 228 stands behind on a Broad Lane short working. *(MMT)*

1958, the other three following early in 1959. These were to be the last front engine buses ordered. Vehicle policy was changing. No more buses were to be ordered for the next two years, but significantly, the Committee had two Leyland Atlantean demonstrators operating on loan at the end of the year.

THE SIXTIES

This decade will be remembered by most people as the swinging sixties; a time when Britain finally broke away from the shackles of rationing and controls. It was an exciting time with new fashions, new designs and new freedoms, but it was also a period when wage inflation started to soar and the viability of the bus industry began to deteriorate. The vicious downward spiral of rising costs, fare increases and loss of passengers, followed by further fare increases, gathered momentum. Services were pruned back but fixed costs remained substantially the same and more income had to be raised from fewer and fewer passengers. Against this background momentous changes would occur which would bring about the end of Rochdale Corporation Transport's independent existence.

During 1960 Mr Cox was investigating the possibility of introducing spray-painting which, coupled with simplification of the livery, would achieve a significant reduction in labour costs. In October one bus was painted in all-over cream with blue mudguards and a single blue band above the lower deck windows. In December a tender of £1,417 was accepted from J and H Lowe (Cranes) Ltd for gantries and other equipment and a spray booth was built in the works.

It was November 1961 before the first re-sprayed buses, one double-deck and one single-deck, were out-shopped, the latter with black mudguards and the blue band under the windows. The deep monestral blue that had served for more than twenty years was replaced by a lighter shade called larkspur. The new simplified livery lent itself better to advertising, and civic pride became the victim of economic necessity. The Council accepted a tender from Frank Mason and Co. Ltd. for interior and exterior advertising for five years, but later resolved not to allow advertising on the outside of the single-deckers. The annual income of £6,172 was enough to purchase a new bus each year. Such was the power of advertising..

At the end of 1961 Mr Cox, who had been General Manager since 1954, resigned to take

Number 321, the penultimate Regent V and one of the four fitted with platform doors, arrives in Bury having worked through from Rochdale via Heywood on service 21. *(MMT)*

In the upper photograph work is in progress on the Mellor Street depot early in 1962 to extend the roof over the open yard. The lower view later in the year shows the completed building. *(Both MMT)*

Three more Reliances with 42-seat two-door bodies by East Lancs were delivered in 1964 to convert the Healey service, which was linked to the existing OMO Wardle route. Initially, both halves of the service were advertised separately as 2/2A between Rochdale and Healey and 7/7A between Rochdale and Wardle, buses showing 2/2A towards Healey and 7/7A towards Wardle. As this caused confusion to passengers, 7/7A was quickly used in both directions. Number 23 stands in Smith Street having worked in from Wardle soon after the service was converted. *(JHC)*

Also new in 1964 were five Daimler Fleetlines with Addlestone-built Weymann bodies to the then standard MCW style. Number 326 is seen at Kay Gardens, the Bury terminus of service 21. *(MMT)*

BIG BUSES

At this time Rochdale's policy was to use single-deck one-man buses on the lighter loaded routes, whilst retaining double-deck crew operation on the more heavily patronised former tram services. In order to achieve savings at peak periods all future double-deck orders were to be high capacity rear-engined vehicles.

The maximum permitted length of double-deck buses had been extended to 30ft in 1956, but for the sake of standardisation Rochdale had continued to purchase 27ft long AEC Regent Vs. During 1959 the Transport Committee had inspected a Leyland Atlantean demonstrator 398JTB and had decided not to take the matter any further, but in July 1961 the Daimler Fleetline demonstrator 7000HP, painted in Birmingham livery, was operated for a short period on the Newhay, Littleborough, Ashton and Bury services. This time the Committee were more impressed and over the next few years Rochdale was to receive 22 Gardner-engined Fleetlines with "Atlantean-type" bodies. The first batch of five, numbered 323-7 (6323-27DK) arrived in March 1964, at a cost of £36,056, with a further seven following in December 1965 as 328-34 (EDK128-34C).

The Regal IVs that had been used on the first one-man conversions were beginning to show their age and in April 1965 the Committee approved the purchase of six more AEC Reliances, but reserved the decision on the bodies until they could examine alternatives. In June they awarded the tender to East Lancashire Coachbuilders, but later switched the order to Willowbrook. Numbered 24-9 (GDK324-9D), they entered service in October 1966.   On 1st July 1966, after a great deal of pressure from the bus operators, the Government had finally authorised one-man operation of double-deck buses and Rochdale's next Fleetlines were suitable for OMO, the most noticeable difference being the design of the front indicator layout which placed the destination box at the bottom of the display so that the blind could be changed by the driver. These ten buses, numbered 335-44 (HDK135-44F), did not arrive until January 1969 and were the last double-deckers to be delivered to Rochdale Corporation. They were also the first double-deckers to be used for one-man operation, but not until SELNEC days when service 21 (Bury) was converted in 1970.

In April 1967, after inspecting Daimler

Number 330, one of the 1965 Fleetlines, stands at the service 21 terminus in the Butts. *(JHC)*

Six further Reliances were delivered in 1966, this time with Loughborough-built Willowbrook bodies. By this time experience had shown that the separate central exit was of no significant value on the type of service being operated, and without it three more seats could be provided. Thus, numbers 24-9 had a front entrance only, 24 being pictured on service 1 to Castleton via Deeplish. It became SELNEC number 6024 and was withdrawn in 1979. *(MMT)*

Fleetline and AEC Swift demonstrators, the Committee ordered a further four of each to replace the last remaining Regal IVs and expand the one-man services. These were four Daimler Fleetlines with Willowbrook bodies numbered 30-3 (LDK830-3G), which were delivered in August 1968 and four AEC Swifts with Pennine bodies from Seddon Motors of Oldham numbered 34-7 (MDK734-7G), which arrived in February 1969. These were the last buses to be delivered before Rochdale's operations passed to the SELNEC Passenger Transport Executive later that year.

THE 1968 TRANSPORT ACT

There had already been three abortive attempts to introduce differing degrees of co-ordination and integration of bus services in the Manchester conurbation; the Joint Committee of the twenties, the SELEC scheme of the thirties and the Area Transport Boards in the forties. These had all fallen by the wayside but in 1964 a Labour Government came to power, committed to an integrated transport system. With the rapid decline in traffic and costs soaring, the time was now more opportune: something had to be done before public transport in Britain followed that of America into near oblivion.

Aware that total nationalisation was no longer a serious political option, attention was focussed on the major conurbations, the one which included Rochdale bearing the ponderous title of "South East Lancashire and North East Cheshire", abbreviated to SELNEC and centred on Manchester. Initially, a small group was set up to look at transport problems and identify possible solutions in the area. Known as the SELNEC Land Use and Transportation Study or SALTS for short, it was largely funded by the Government with contributions from the constituent local authorities.

In 1965 the Minister of Transport, Mrs Barbara Castle, produced a White Paper called 'Transport Policy' proposing the creation of a number of

Rochdale's last buses delivered before the undertakings' absorption into SELNEC were all single-deckers, four Daimler Fleetlines and four AEC Swifts, which replaced the remaining Regal IVs. In the upper picture Fleetline number 32 carries a Willowbrook body that, with a redesigned front end, looks more modern than No 24 which was only two years older. Number 32, later SELNEC 6032, saw further service from Bolton depot before being withdrawn in 1980 and passing to the Wythenshawe Community Trust. *(JHC)*
Pictured below in Smith Street while working through from Wardle to Healey, number 35, a locally Pennine-bodied AEC Swift delivered in February 1969, became SELNEC 6035 and was also withdrawn in 1980. *(RM)*

Conurbation Transport Authorities to plan, manage and finance the operation of local transport within their areas. They would also be responsible for land use and highway planning and even car parking policy. While Rochdale, like most other local authorities, accepted the need for some form of integration, and indeed amalgamation, they were unhappy about an outside body being able to set service levels and fares without consultation, exactly the same reason that the SELEC scheme had foundered some thirty years earlier.

After lengthy consultation a further White Paper, *Public Transport and Planning*, was produced in 1967. This proposed a two-tier organisation with a Passenger Transport Authority, consisting of elected members of the constituent authorities, to set policy and a professional Passenger Transport Executive to carry it out. The Executive would acquire the assets of the local authorities and would operate the services. The White Paper became the 1968 Transport Act, which came into force on 1st April 1969, a date that its critics deemed appropriate, and the Passenger Transport Authority took over.

SERVICE REVISIONS

After the one-manning of the Healey service in 1965 it had been decided not to implement any further major conversions for the present. New single-deck buses were used to replace the ageing and generally unsuitable Regal IVs and service revisions were confined to serving areas of new housing and the continuous search for economies.

One such economy was the linking of services 11A/11C (Norden) with 18 (Kirkholt). As usual, both legs were licenced and advertised as separate services but by now it had become commonplace on peak hour workings to show the ultimate service number and destination if a bus changed from one route to another in the town centre, but now, the practice was extended to a frequent all-day service with buses showing 11A (via Spotland Road) and 11C (via Mellor Street) on journeys to Norden, but 18 (via Mellor Street) and 18A (via Spotland Road) on journeys to Kirkholt. Luckily, the travelling public of Rochdale were never particularly concerned about service numbers, usually referring simply to 'the Syke bus' or 'the Norden bus'.

In the summer of 1965 AEC Regent V number 290 leans over as it swings round the roundabout at the bottom of Yorkshire Street on its way to Norden on service 11A. *(MMT)*

Service 14 between Greave and Kingsway had been considered for eventual conversion to OMO in the last couple of years of municipal operation, but this did not happen and the route remained conductor-operated until it disappeared in SELNEC's restructuring of the Norden services much later. These two scenes on the route show *(upper)* Daimler CVG6 No 238 turning out of Oldham Road into Kingsway at the start of its journey to Greave and *(lower)* AEC Regent V No 280 crossing the bottom of Drake Street into South Parade. The Fleetline in the background has just left its stop in Smith Street and will turn left up Drake Street on its was to Newhay. *(Both MMT)*

AEC Regent V number 284 passes the Mellor Street offices on its way from Norden to Kirkholt during the short period when buses showed 18 towards Kirkholt and 11 towards Norden. *(MMT)*

Requests for new services were considered. Some, such as the Clay Lane estate in Norden, the Ladyhouse area of Milnrow and Roch Valley Way were turned down. Ironically, all three were later introduced, either by SELNEC or its successors, and still operate in some form today. Early in 1965 service 9A (Kirkholt) was extended further along Hill Top Drive from Friars Crescent to Kirkholt Flats as 9C and a service was introduced to the new Smallbridge estate off Halifax Road. This was a cross-town extension of service 12A (Daniel Fold) and was routed via John Street and Halifax Road.

On 2nd May 1966 Manchester Corporation's long-standing service 4 (Manchester-Bamford) was extended back to its original terminus at Norden. At Norden War Memorial a separate bus stop was erected, some distance from the Rochdale stop with its shelter, labelled 'Manchester service 4' in red letters. At the same time one journey an hour on service 5 (Bamford via Bury Road) was linked to the hourly 4 (Bamford via Mellor Street), which was then routed along Spotland Road and renumbered 4A.

COUNTDOWN

Consultation was well advanced on the White Paper but, although time was ticking slowly towards its inevitable conclusion, the job still had to go on.

During 1967 construction had begun on the Ashfield Valley estate, a complex of deck access flats located either side of the Sudden Brook, to the north of Queensway. Originally, there had been a lane crossing the valley here and it was intended

that this would become a through road linking both halves of the estate. A one-man service was planned following a circular route along Oldham Road and Queensway then through the estate to Ashfield Road and back to Rochdale via the railway station. It would then be extended across the town centre to provide a service to another new development of high-rise blocks at College Bank.

However, conscious that it would be used as a rat run, the scheme for the through road was abandoned and with it the service to the south side of the estate which was close to Queensway.

The service commenced in 1969 running in two parts as 22 Rochdale and Ashfield Road (Arundel Street) and 23 Rochdale and College Bank (Holland Street) although operated by the same bus. It had a somewhat chequered history before disappearing completely when the estate itself was largely demolished after a life of less than thirty years.

THE LAST MONTHS

The Passenger Transport Authority came into being on 1st April 1969 and while for the time being the Council remained responsible for day-to-day operation, all policy and planning matters were passed to the Authority. Outwardly, things went on as usual.

In November 1968 Mr Proctor had recommended the purchase of a further twenty new single-deck buses. The Committee invited tenders but, with an eye to the future, they sought the opinion of the Ministry of Transport on the question of loan sanction. In May 1969 the Ministry approved in

Regent V number 310 stands at Kay Gardens, Bury, before leaving for Rochdale on service 21. *(STA)*

AEC Reliance number 20 is pictured in a wet Smith Street after arriving from Wardle on service 7. *(STA)*

principle the purchase of the new buses and orders were placed for ten AEC Swifts and ten Daimler Fleetlines, all with Pennine 42-seat two-door single-deck bodies. The orders were taken over by SELNEC and the ten Swifts were delivered to the PTE in 1971/72. The Fleetline order was changed dramatically, the buses becoming prototypes for the new SELNEC standard double-decker.

In August 1969 the Committee approved the purchase of a Willowbrook-bodied Daimler Fleetline demonstrator that was on loan and operating in Rochdale colours carrying fleet number 38 (KKV700G). The transaction was not completed until after SELNEC took control and the vehicle never officially belonged to Rochdale Corporation.

A commemorative function marking the transfer of the undertaking to the Passenger Transport Authority took place on 23rd October, attended by Councillors, Chief Officers, Chairmen and Managers of joint operators and selected employees and members of staff. Finally, on 1st November 1969 the SELNEC Passenger Transport Executive took over the eleven municipal operators in its area, bringing to an end

67 years of municipally owned public transport in Rochdale. The Passenger Transport Committee was disbanded and responsibility for the few matters remaining passed to the General Purposes Committee.

INTO SELNEC

Things did not change overnight. The PTE organised the eleven former municipal bus undertakings into three divisions, Northern, Central and Southern, Rochdale becoming a District of the Northern Division, which had its headquarters in the former Bolton Corporation Transport head office in Bradshawgate. In addition to Rochdale and Bolton it also included Bury, Ramsbottom and Leigh.

The first outward sign of things to come was the new Sunglow Orange and White livery which started to appear on the buses in the following March. At the same time SELNEC's new logo, a stylised 'S' together with the divisional name, was applied to all buses, whether repainted or not and, more controversially, the existing municipal coats of arms were removed from the vehicle

On a typical wet northern afternoon number 335, one of the final batch of Fleetlines, heads north out of Ashton along Oldham Road on its way home to Rochdale. The revised indicator layout allowed drivers to change the destination from the cab, making the vehicles suitable for one-man operation, although they were never used as such until SELNEC took over. *(MMT)*

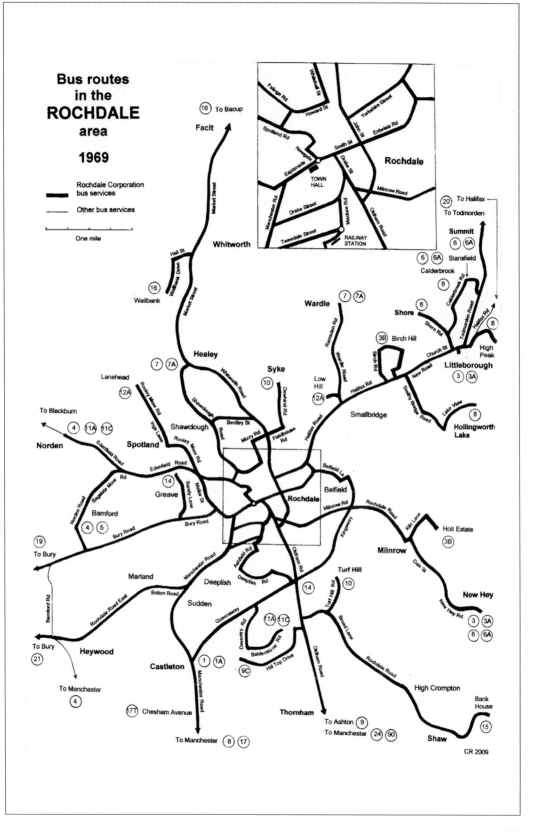

Bus routes in the ROCHDALE area

1969

Rochdale Corporation bus services

Other bus services

One mile

16 To Bacup

Facit

Market Street

Whitworth

Hall St

Wailbank Drive

16

Wailbank

Market Street

Healey

7 7A

Lanehead

12A

Rooley Moor Rd

Inys Lane

To Blackburn

4 11A 11C

Norden

Edenfield Road

Bagslate Moor Rd

Norden Road

Spotland

Edenfield Road

Melbor St

Sandy Lane

14

Greave

Bamford

4 5

Bury Road

19

To Bury

Bamford Rd

Marland

Rochdale Road East

Bolton Road

Manchester Road

Deeplish

Deeplish Rd

Sudden

Queensway

Daventry Rd

Balderstone Rd

Hill Top Drive

To Bury

21

Heywood

To Manchester

4

Castleton

1 1A

9C

Manchester Road

17T Chesham Avenue

To Manchester 8 17

Shawclough

Shawclough Road

Bentley St

Mizzy Rd

Fieldhouse Rd

Whitworth Road

Dewhirst Rd

Syke

10

Low Hill

12A

Halifax Road

Halifax Rd

Wardle Road

Ramsden Rd

Wardle

7 7A

3B Birch Hill

Birch Hill Rd

Smallbridge

Smithy Bridge Road

New Road

Church St

Shore Rd

8

Shore

8

Stansfield

6 6A

Calderbrook

8

Calderbrook Rd

Todmorden Road

Halifax Rd

8

High Peak

Littleborough

3 3A

Lake View

8

Hollingworth Lake

Rochdale

Belfield La

Belfield

Milnrow Rd

Rochdale Road

Kiln Lane

Holt Estate

3B

Milnrow

Dale St

New Hey

New Hey Rd

3 3A

6 6A

Kingsway

Oldham Rd

Turf Hill

10

Turf Hill Rd

14

Broad Lane

Oldham Road

Rochdale Road

High Crompton

Bank House

15

Shaw

Thornham

To Ashton 9

To Manchester 24 90

Summit

6 6A

20 To Halifax

To Todmorden

CR 2009

Daimler Fleetline number 6224, formerly 324, was the first Rochdale bus to be painted into the new SELNEC orange and white colours. One bus from each of the constituent operators was painted at the end of 1969 and 6224 displays the new livery for the media on the Hyde Road training school yard. *(MMT)*

sides. Rochdale buses gained a magenta 'lazy S' with the name 'Northern' in black. The next step was to introduce a unified fleet numbering scheme, Northern Division buses being renumbered between 6001 and 6999. Rochdale's single-deckers 16-38 became 6016 to 6038 and the double-deckers 238-344 became 6138 to 6244. The new numbers were applied haphazardly and in different styles of lettering dependant upon what was available at the time, although it all got sorted out eventually with black numerals being applied on repainting.

The oldest buses, the first Daimler CVG6s were withdrawn in 1970 and within three years all 30 had gone, none of them receiving the orange livery. The ten Pennine-bodied AEC Swifts ordered by the Corporation entered service in 1971/72 in SELNEC livery, numbered 6040-9 (TDK540-3J and TDK544-9K) in the Northern Division single-deck series. Eventually, they all gravitated to Leigh where they remained until

withdrawal in 1981, most seeing further use with small independent operators.

But a different and far more interesting fate befell the ten single-deck Fleetlines. From the beginning the PTE had made no secret of its intention to develop a standard double-deck bus and, to this end, some of the outstanding orders inherited from different constituent undertakings were modified by SELNEC's engineers as prototypes of the new design, Rochdale's single-deckers emerging in 1972 as double-deckers. Numbered in the PTE experimental series, EX7-11 (TNB747-51K) carried Northern Counties single-door bodies, while EX17-21 (TNB757-61K) had similar two-door bodies. After evaluation, mainly on former Manchester service 53, they came home to Rochdale in 1974 and were renumbered 6245-54 immediately following the last of Rochdale's own double-deckers. They stayed at Rochdale until their withdrawal in 1984/5 and 6252 is preserved.

Behind the scenes a lot of work was carried out into standardisation of wages, conditions and operating practices, most of which went unnoticed by the general public, although a necessary but unfortunately timed 15% fare increase did not. More obvious was the comprehensive service-numbering scheme. Initially, services had continued to show the numbers used by their former operators and it was not until 1972 that SELNEC developed a single unified scheme. Renumbering was implemented in stages over several months starting in November 1972. Rochdale was the last area to be completed in April 1974, most of its services being numbered in the 400 block.

As one-man operation increased and new standard buses were delivered, older vehicles were moved around, resulting in a number of the Regent Vs, by now the only former Rochdale half-cab buses remaining, passing to Oldham and the Manchester depots, to be replaced by new standards. But more changes were in the pipeline.

Rochdale's last order, initially for ten Daimler Fleetline single-deckers, arrived in 1972 as prototypes for SELNEC's standard double-decker, five each with single- and dual-door bodies. The latter batch worked from Manchester's Hyde Road garage and EX17 is seen (above) in Hyde on the 210 service to Gee Cross. In 1973 EX20 (right) received SELNEC's first all-over advertising livery, for Barclaycard, and displays its striking blue, white and orange livery as it travels along Manchester's Thompson Street past the former Lancashire and Yorkshire Railway's Oldham Road goods depot on the long cross-city 112 route from Sale to Moston. (both JAS)

GREATER MANCHESTER

As a result of the 1973 Local Government Act the SELNEC Passenger Transport Authority was abolished and overall transport strategy came directly under the control of the newly formed Greater Manchester Council from 1st April 1974. The bus and rail operations became the Greater Manchester PTE with a new 'wiggly M' logo and the title 'Greater Manchester Transport'.

Outwardly, however, this was the only change. The first Regent Vs had been withdrawn as early as 1971, but many survived for much longer. The last six, 6179/98, 6203/8/9/22 went in 1977, bringing to an end the long line of rear platform half-cab double-deckers which had started in 1930 with number 37, the first Crossley Condor. Two examples are preserved, 6180 at Boyle Street and 6222, numerically the last, at the South Yorkshire Transport Museum.

May 1978 saw the opening of Rochdale's new £4.3 million bus station, which had 24 bus stands beneath a 570-space multi-story car park. The bus station was on an island site between Smith St and Baillie St, and subways and escalators provided access to the central shopping area. From the start there were persistent complaints in the local press of fumes, draughts and escalators not working. Many writers bemoaned the loss of the town centre stops, but to anyone who had had to endure a five minute walk in pouring rain from the Post Office to Smith St when changing buses, the covered interchange was a godsend.

In 1980 GMT introduced a new livery retaining orange as the main body colour but with a white roof and upper deck window surrounds and a brown skirt. Further re-organisation of the management structure in 1981 created four areas, North, South, East and West, Rochdale becoming part of the new North area along with Bury, Queens Road (Manchester) and the former Salford depots at Frederick Road and Weaste and, together with the other districts, was reduced to depot status, decision-making being concentrated in the new Northern Division headquarters at Frederick Road, Salford. The same year the last Rochdale buses, Fleetlines 6223/5, were withdrawn.

6245-54, the prototype standard double-deckers, which were the last Rochdale order, were withdrawn in 1985 and in 1991 Rochdale depot itself closed and the operation was transferred to other Greater Manchester depots at Oldham, Bury and Queens Road, Manchester.

THE PRESENT DAY

The only remaining trace of Rochdale Corporation's once proud Transport Department, which had provided tram and bus services in the Borough and surrounding districts for 66 years, is the former depot and offices in Mellor Street. A vegetable distribution company now occupies the depot and the ornate red brick offices, but the workshops across the road have been demolished.

Since the break up and subsequent privatisation of Greater Manchester Buses, First Group, through its subsidiaries First Manchester and First West Yorkshire, runs the longer distance routes out of the town, together with a handful of local services. Rossendale Transport took over many local routes, which were given up by First Manchester and now has its own depot in Rochdale. The third local operator, Bu-Val, runs a number of mainly GMITE supported services from a depot at Smithy Bridge.

Buses of Stagecoach Manchester and Middleton operators Bluebird and JP Travel can also be seen in the town, but the blue and cream Corporation Bus is now just a memory.

The Corporation Transport department is no more and SELNEC Fleetline number 6242, formerly Rochdale 342, turns its back on the town centre and climbs up Drake Street on its way to Newhay. *(MMT)*

Following the demise of the Transport Department, Rochdale's buses were renumbered into SELNEC's 6xxx block and gradually repainted into the new orange and white livery with Northern Division magenta logos on their sides. Most former Rochdale buses spent the remainder of their working lives in the town, one being AEC Regent V number 6183, formerly Rochdale 283, which is pictured *(above)* in South Parade on service 11A to Norden. However, a handful of them were transferred away to other depots to make way for new one-man buses. In the lower picture a pair of Regent Vs stand in the former Oldham Corporation depot at Walshaw Street, ready to go out on evening peak duties. *(Both MMT)*

Number 13, the last of the 1935 batch of Leyland TS8s with Eastern Coach Works bodies, stands outside the General Post Office before working a service 1 journey to Castleton. Behind, number 173, an ECW-bodied Leyland TD7, has just arrived from Broad Lane. *(PDC)*

Smith Street on a Saturday afternoon in the forties. Passengers alight from an Austerity Daimler that has just arrived from Littleborough while number 180, an ECW-bodied Daimler COG6, stands behind on an extra. In the background 136, a Cravens-bodied AEC Regent is working a special to Rochdale Football Club's ground at Spotland. *(STA)*

Upper Two more Eastern Coach Works-bodied buses, Daimler COG6 number 186 of 1940 and Leyland TD5 number 148 dating from 1938, stand on the bus park. Most of the buildings in the picture have been obliterated by the Wheatsheaf shopping centre and the bus station, but the somewhat run-down premises of the Bradford Equitable Building Society still stand, although the building is now a wine bar. *(PDC)*

Lower. Also on the bus park in 1956, number 121, the 1935 AEC Regent rebodied by Samlesbury in 1951, has only a few months remaining before being withdrawn and meanwhile has been relegated to driver training. It was sold to Bee Line of West Hartlepool and was later owned by a Middlesbrough contractor, before being broken up in 1960 after a life of 25 years. *(STA)*

This page. The Town Hall Square was long a favourite location for official photographs of new buses. Massey-bodied Daimler CWD6 number 21, Rochdale's first post-war bus, stands round the back of the Town Hall in November 1945, showing off its pristine paintwork. The somewhat stark slopes of Broadfield Park in the background are now covered with mature trees. *(MMT)*

Opposite page upper. In May 1944, Duple austerity-bodied CWA6 number 193 stands in the square proper. St. Chad's Parish Church looms out of the mist in the background. *(RLS)*

Opposite page lower. A more sunny view. Number 29, one of the Daimlers with an AEC engine, stands on the Smith Street bus park. Despite the drawbacks of poor materials in the immediate post-war period, this bus survived until March 1959. *(RM)*

This 1952 line up comprises 1940 ECW-bodied Leyland TD5 number 173, former Sheffield Weymann-bodied AEC Regent 72, Weymann-bodied AEC Regent III 42, Samlesbury re-bodied AEC Regent 125 and another, unidentified, Regent III. *(MMT)*

The first Weymann-bodied AEC Regent IIIs, delivered in 1947 and 1948, lasted until 1963/64. Number 32 of the 1947 batch and Nos. 38 and 42 of the 1948 batch line-up on the bus park between peak hour duties. *(PDC)*

Three generations of Weymann-bodied AEC Regents stand on the bus park. From left to right they are 1948 7ft 6in Regent III number 42 1950 8ft Regent III No. 227 and 1956 Regent V No 280, which is now preserved at Greater Manchester's Museum of Transport in Boyle Street, Manchester. *(MMT)*

A brace of Daimlers stands on the bus park. Numbers 245 and 262 survived to become SELNEC's 6145 and 6162 and were not withdrawn until 1971. *(JHC)*

The first of the AEC Reliances, numbers 16-20, (upper photograph) had two-door 42-seat bodies by Weymann, but the second door was not justified on the services for which they were used. Replacing the middle door by a plain panel in subsequent buses like Willowbrook bodied No 26 (lower) saved a considerable amount of money and allowed for a further three seats. *(MMT)*

In the 1960s Turners Asbestos was the biggest employer in Rochdale. Here AEC Regents Nos. 209 and 42 wait at the Royds Arms on Rooley Moor Road to take workers home. Note how the extra six inches width changes the looks of the otherwise identical Weymann bodies on the two buses. *(MMT)*

A handsome 1948 Weymann-bodied Regent III stands in Smith Street, ready to leave for Manchester on the former Yelloway express service 24. *(JHC)*

One of the second batch of Daimler CVG6s, number 258, stands in Smith Street on the Kingsway stop. In the background is the Regal Cinema and over the fence behind the shelter is the site of the former Kelsall and Kemp's mill, which is now occupied by the bus station. *(MMT)*

Number 275, a 1956 Weymann-bodied AEC Regent V stands on the opposite side of Smith Street on its way from Littleborough to Newhay. The building behind is now unoccupied and in the background the Electric House, originally the showrooms and offices of the former National Electricity Board, has been demolished to make room for the new transport interchange. *(STA)*

Before entering service buses have to pass a test to check how far they can tilt before going over. These two pictures show Daimler CVG6 No 239 and Fleetline No 325 undertaking the test at Chiswick where London Transport undertook such work for Weymann's and several other bodybuilders. *(both STA)*

INSIDE AND OUT

In the upper picture AEC Regent III No 38 poses outside the AEC factory before delivery to Rochdale in January 1948, the camera angle emphasising the classic lines of the post-war Weymann body. *(STA).*
The lower view shows the less often photographed, but equally well-known interior of the lower deck of number 43 of the same type, showing the white ceiling, oak framing around the window, the dark blue panelling and seat backs and the large Clayton Dewandre saloon heater on the front bulkhead. There is also a notice saying that conductors are wanted. Note that, although the body was built in Addlestone by Weymann, the transmission housing shows MCW, the joint Metro-Cammell/Weymann sales organisation. (JHC)

One of the second batch of Regal IVs, Burlingham bodied number 10, (originally 310), has just left its stop outside the General Post Office and crossed the end of Newgate on its way to Castleton, passing Barclays Bank which is being refurbished. *(PDC).* The interior of No 10, below, shows detailed difference in treatment from 43. In the intervening years the oak window surrounds have given way to alloy and there is more white, giving a much lighter impression. The bus has been modified for one-man-operation and there is a stopping sign on the cab bulkhead, but conductors are still wanted. Some things didn't change. *(JHC)*

ACCIDENTS

Fortunately, serious accidents were rare, but some were spectacular. In the upper photograph in June 1935, a Ribble bus travelling from Rochdale to Burnley lies on its side at Temple Lane on the climb to Littleborough Summit after the steering apparently failed. The driver braked but the bus skidded on the wet cobbles, hit a lamp standard and overturned. The driver, conductor and two passengers were taken to Rochdale Infirmary but suffered only minor injuries. *(RO)*

The commuters on their morning express journey to Manchester would have been late for work when AEC Regent III number 218 *(below)* skidded on the wet surface of Drake Street, demolished the corner of a shop and careered across Trafford Street to end up embedded in the wall of a building opposite. *(MMT)*

Spotland Bridge on the morning of 26th April 1955. A Regent III, working the 07.00 11A from Norden to Rochdale ran through the stop line at the bottom of Edenfield Road and smashed into the side of Daimler CWA6 number 191 on the 07.05 service 12A from Rochdale to Daniel Fold, pushing it into the window of Whitehead's shop on Rooley Moor Road. Twenty-six passengers and a driver and conductor were taken to hospital, luckily none suffering serious injuries. Number 191 was written off and was used to give the breakdown crew training in righting overturned buses before being sold for scrap. *(both RO)*

In 1951 several buses received new bodies as their original ones were worn out. Number 198, a Daimler CWA6 dating from 1944, is pictured *(top)* with its Northern Counties austerity body and *(bottom)* with the 1940 Eastern Coach Works body it obtained from No 185. *(both PDC)*

On the opposite page, number 120, the first AEC to join the fleet in September 1935, is pictured *(top)* in its original condition with a 52-seat Metro-Cammell body prior to delivery *(STA)*, while in the lower picture it stands in Packer Street showing off its new 7ft 9" Samlesbury body. *(JHC)*

JOINT OPERATION

There was much joint operation throughout the Greater Manchester area, and Rochdale at various times ran jointly with seven other operators. In the upper photograph, taken in early 1946, new Massey-bodied Daimler CWD6 number 23 stands at the spartan shelter in Manchester's Cannon Street while working the long service 17. At this time the Manchester buses on the route would normally be pre-war Leyland TD5s from Queens Road depot, but occasionally a new Crossley would be turned out. *(JHC)*

Service 9 to Oldham and Ashton was worked jointly by buses of all three Corporations. The boundary between the Rochdale and Oldham areas was at Thornham Summit where two AEC Regent Vs wait their time in the lower photograph, taken in 1965. *(RLS)*

Joint operation also brought other operators' buses into Rochdale on a reciprocal basis. In post-war years Manchester and North Western's bright red, Ashton's lighter blue, Bury and Todmorden's different greens, Oldham's crimson lake and Ribble's maroon brought contrasting colours to the town centre, as well as different makes of chassis and bodywork.

Top. The Rochdale terminus of the 17 service was outside the Midland Bank at the bottom of Yorkshire Street. The crew of Manchester Corporation's 1951 Metro-Cammell-bodied Leyland PD2/6 number 3231 stand chatting in the rain in this early 1960s picture. By this time these buses were unusual visitors to Rochdale, Manchester's workings being normally covered by much newer Leylands. *(STA)*

Middle. Bury's 1950 Leyland PD2/4 number 170 carries a Weymann body similar to those on Rochdale's AEC Regents of the same period, although the different colour, cab front and indicator arrangements would make them appear quite different to the casual onlooker. The bus stands in Packer Street at the terminus of service 19 to Bury via Jericho. *(STA)*

Bottom. Ashton under Lyne's number 17, a Leyland PD2/12 with body by Crossley dating from 1955, stands outside the General Post Office opposite the Town Hall on service 9. The Rochdale Daimler CVG6 behind is on service 18 to Kirkholt and will follow the same route as far as Queensway. *(STA)*

NEW OWNERS

A number of buses went on to work for other operators after being withdrawn from service in Rochdale. Leyland TD5 number 147, dating from 1938, was withdrawn in 1954 and purchased by North Western Road Car for use as a staff canteen and is pictured below in that role at Manchester's Lower Mosley Street bus station. NWRC was a lowbridge operator until the arrival of Lolines and Fleetlines and thus had nothing suitable from its own fleet. *(MTMS)*

Massey-bodied Daimlers 21 and 25 of 1945 went to Leon Motor Services of Finningley near Doncaster where number 21 is shown (bottom) while 25 is just visible in the background. *(MMT)*

Number 122 was a 1936 AEC Regent, originally with an English Electric body, which received a new 7ft 9in wide Samlesbury body in 1951. It was withdrawn in 1957 and saw further service with Bee Line of West Hartlepool, on whose premises it is seen below, still in Rochdale's colours. *(JHC)*

AEC Regent III number 230 was new to Rochdale in March 1950. It was withdrawn in January 1968 and sold to Prospect Coaches of Lye in the West Midlands, with whom it was photographed in the bottom picture, again still in its Rochdale livery. *(JHC)*

ROCHDALE BUSES PRESERVED

Four Rochdale buses, all AEC Regents, are known to be preserved, three of which are featured here. East Lancashire-bodied Regent III number 235 is privately owned and is shown in the upper picture parked on the Town Hall Square in 1972. Weymann-bodied Regent V number 322 (lower), the last front-engined rear-entrance bus delivered to Rochdale and the last painted from new in the old livery' is now housed at the South Yorkshire Transport Museum at Rotherham. *(upper JAS, lower PDC)*

Number 280, a 1956 Weymann-bodied AEC Regent V stands on display in Greater Manchester's Museum of Transport in Boyle Street, Manchester. On the right is a former Manchester City Transport Crossley double-decker. (*JAS*)

THEN AND NOW

Forty-three years separate these two photographs taken at the Odeon stop on Drake Street. In the upper picture Weymann-bodied AEC Regent III number 221, on a service 17T journey to Castleton, pulls out to overtake similar 228 working a peak hour short journey on service 21 sometime in the spring of 1966. (JHC)

Below, in September 2009, a First Manchester Wright-bodied Volvo B9TL approaches the same stop on a service 17 journey to Manchester. The Odeon has long gone as, more recently, has the retail estate that took its place, and the proposed Metrolink tram stop will eventually be located between the pavement and the line of fencing in the background. (CR)

The scene at the bottom of Drake Street is little changed in the 50 years between this pair of pictures. In 1958 (above), before town centre redevelopment, Drake Street was a prosperous shopping street and the Manchester Corporation Metro-Cammell-bodied Leyland PD2/40 arriving in town on service 17 was turning left to its terminus on The Butts. *(RLS)*

In 2008 Drake Street is waiting for Metrolink to rejuvenate it and the First Manchester Volvo is about to turn right towards the bus station. (CR)

The trees have grown in the intervening years, but otherwise this scene in Long Street, Middleton, is unchanged in half a century. In the scene above two-year old Weymann-bodied AEC Regent V, number 276 drops down the hill past Jubilee Park on its way to Manchester on service 17. *(MMT)*

In the spring of 2008, with blossom on the trees, another First Manchester Volvo is caught by the camera in exactly the same spot. Even the service number is the same. (CR)

If the previous pairs of photographs can be easily identified as of the same place, those on this page cannot look more different. In 1958 (above) an East Lancs-bodied Regent III has come down from Syke and is about to turn right from St. Mary's Gate into Blackwater Street on its way across town to Turf Hill. In the background Bury Road bears left and Spotland Road curves away uphill to the right. *(RLS)*

Fifty years later everything has been swept away, tower blocks have replaced the old mills and terraced houses and the road pattern is completely changed. In the lower picture, taken from the identical location, St. Mary's Gate has been submerged by the dual-carriageway ring road and a Rossendale Transport Optare Solo turns out of a re-aligned Spotland Road on what is now service 440. (CR)

Great changes are taking place as AEC Regent V number 269 travels along Newgate on the cross-town Norden to Kirkholt service. By the late sixties the use of 18/18A on journeys towards Kirkholt had been discontinued and buses showed 11A/11C in both directions. This part of Newgate is a wasteland as everything has been demolished to make way for the huge new shopping centre. *(JHC)*

ROCHDALE IN COLOUR

On a cold winter's day Willowbrook-bodied Daimler Fleetline number 38 turns at Bank House, the terminus of service 15 up the hill beyond Shaw. Although painted in Rochdale's blue and cream, 38 never belonged to the Corporation. It was a Daimler demonstrator and was purchased by SELNEC in February 1970. *(JHC)*
In early SELNEC days Regent V number 312, now carrying SELNEC number 6212, is still in Rochdale livery as it stands in Manchester's Stevenson Square on service 24. Also in the picture are two Oldham and one Manchester Leylands, also in their previous owners' colours. (STA)

Above. East Lancs-bodied AEC Regal IV number 6 stands in the Town Hall Square on one-man operated service 5 to Bamford Village. *(JHC)*

Below. Weymann-bodied AEC Regent III number 226 is pictured on the bus park. *(STA)*

Left. An AEC Regent V in its original colour scheme, number 313 on Oldham Road, *en route* to Ashton on service 9. *(PDC)*

Below. Another Regent V, this time 279 in the post-1961 livery stands outside the General Post Office. The new police station is rising up in the background on the far side of the Memorial Gardens. *(PDC)*

Two more views of the Smith Street bus park. The line up above comprises East Lancs-bodied AEC Regal IV number 2, Weymann-bodied AEC Regent III 42 and Weymann-bodied Daimler CVG6 267 resting between duties, *(APY)*. In the lower picture another Daimler, No 259, stands alone with Penn Street Chapel in the background across Bailey Street. *(JHC)*

Two views of Rochdale buses in Bury. In the upper picture Regent V number 302 arrives in the town at the end of its journey on service 19, the final development of the early Cemetery to Jericho route. Below, Fleetline number 340, one of the last order designed for one-man operation, stands at the Kay Gardens terminus before leaving for Rochdale on service 21. *(both JHC)*

This line-up on the Smith Street bus park shows the variety of liveries that still existed in the early seventies, including both Rochdale Corporation and SELNEC, together with three Yelloway coaches. *(APY)*

Pennine-bodied AEC Swift number 34, now SELNEC 6034, pauses in the town centre while working a service 7A journey from Healey to Wardle. In the background a Regent V stands on the service 17 stop outside the Midland Bank. (JAS)

AEC Regent V number 6206, formerly Rochdale 306, is about to leave on service 17 to Manchester. A former Manchester Corporation Leyland PD2/37 stands behind. *(JAS)*

Daimler Fleetline 6229, once 329, stands in Kay Gardens, Bury on service 21 which was shortly to become Rochdale's first double-deck one-man operated route. The front destination box has already been moved to the bottom of the display to allow the driver to change the indicator without leaving the cab, (STA)

The last trace of Rochdale's once extensive tramway network is this short stretch of track preserved in traditional setts on the former line of Yorkshire Street at Townhead. *(CR)*

The inn sign of the Oxford Inn, the original terminus of the Whitworth Road trams at the Oxford loop, Healey, depicts what purports to be a Rochdale tram. *(CR)*

In May 2009 little remains of the Mellor Street workshops as the demolition gang moves in. *(CR)*

The bus garage *(above),* now occupied by a vegetable wholesaler and the offices *(below),* now home to several small firms, are all that remain of the long gone Passenger Transport Department. *(CR)*

APPENDIX 1 - ROCHDALE TICKETS

The examples on the next two pages are from the collection of Brian Hughes and show the basic three stages in ticket development from early Bell Punch types carried in a hand-held wooden rack and validated with a manual punch, through the pre-printed Ultimate rolls issued from a portable machine and validated with the stage number by a carbon strip, to tickets printed directly on to paper rolls.

Pre-printed tickets carried unique identifying numbers and had to be accounted for on a waybill at the end of a shift and takings paid in accordingly. Where a large variety of tickets were carried, as on jointly operated routes., this could take some time. Ticket issuing machines, on the other hand simply counted up the total cash value and reduced accounting time virtually to zero.

Details of the tickets illustrated are as follows:

Z4000	Geographical workman's ticket (Rochdale Corporation Tramways) issued on the Heywood service.
H 4074	Numerical stage ticket (Rochdale Corporation Tramways).
LW1120	Numerical ten-stage (Rochdale Corporation Passenger Transport Dept).
BW8924	Numerical seven-stage ticket (Rochdale Corporation Transport). The final design of Bell Punch ticket.
2883	Numerical stage workman's return ticket overprinted with day identifier.
O1046	Early morning return ticket (RCT)
A9764	Return ticket issued on express services. Note that it includes geographical stages for both Walsden and Urmston.
K5065	Return ticket for the Todmorden route.
A0688	Child return, also for the Todmorden route.
A5348	Numerical 24-stage ticket
C0619	Return ticket with dates.
B5167	Seven-stage ticket.
AO0631	Single through fare to Manchester.
B6428	Single through fare to Bury overprinted JOINT (Rochdale and Bury) issued by both Rochdale and Bury.
RE5402	Single through fare to Manchester (Manchester and Rochdale) issued by Manchester.
4366	TIM ticket with special print plate to celebrate the centenary of Rochdale Borough.
KT21195	Ultimate type double ticket
SA44439	Ultimate type double decimal ticket issued by Rochdale District (SELNEC).
04825	Ultimate type souvenir issued on Rochdale Corporation bus visiting Rochdale's twin town of Turcoing.
N5929	Ashton and Oldham crossover ticket on service 9.
K5866	Rochdale and Oldham crossover ticket on service 9.
A3939	Double crossover ticket on service 9.
F0716	Rochdale and Oldham crossover ticket on service 9.
H0196	Geographical crossover ticket between Royton Town Hall and Ashton.
2018	Ashton, Oldham and Rochdale geographical return ticket with dates.
0230	Token issued to Gas Board employees to purchase tickets.
23392	Token issued to schoolchildren to purchase tickets.
A9834	Parcels receipt.
364	Almex ticket issued by SELNEC

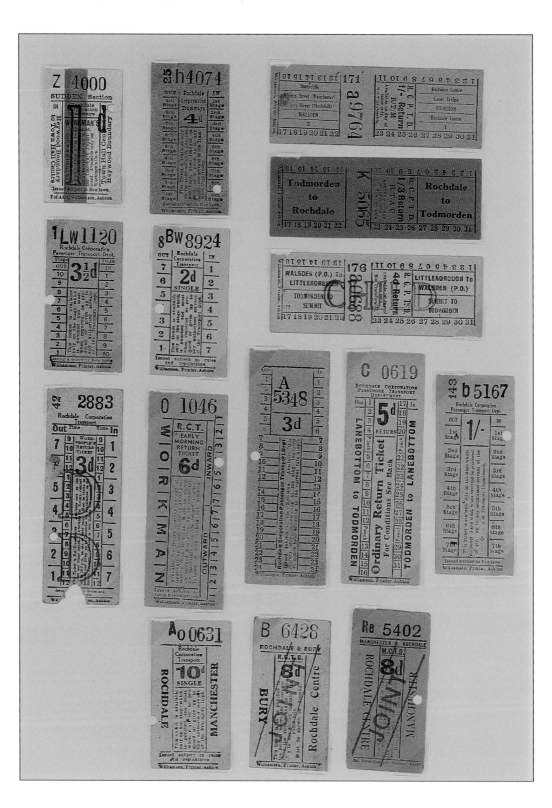

APPENDIX 2 – TRAM FLEET LIST

YEAR	FLEET Nos.	TYPE	TRUCKS	BODY
1902	1	Single-deck bogie	Brill 22E	ERTCW
1902	2	Open-top bogie	Brill 22E	ERTCW
1902	3	Open top 4-wheelBrill 21E	ERTCW	
1902	4	Open-top bogie	Brush D	Milnes
1902	5	Open-top bogie	Brush B	Milnes
1902	6	Open-top bogie	Brush D	Milnes
1902	7-9	Open-top 4-wheel	Brill 21E	ERTCW
1903	10-19	Open-top 4-wheel	Brush AA	Brush
1905	20-29	Open-top 4-wheel	Brush Radial	Brush
1905	30-43	Single-deck bogie	Brush D	Brush
1905	44-49	Open-top bogie	Brush D	Brush
1906	50-59	Single-deck bogie	Brush D	Brush
1912	60-69	Single-deck bogie	Brush D	Brush
1920	70-79	Balcony 4-wheel	Brill 21E	English Electric
1925	2, 12-15	Open-top 4-wheel	Brush Radial	Brush
1925-26	80-89	Enclosed 4-wheel	Preston 21E	English Electric
1926	90-92	Enclosed 4-wheel	Brill 21E	English Electric
1927-28	93-94	Enclosed 4-wheel	Brill 21E	RCT

2, 12-15 came from the Middleton Electric Traction Company, built 1905.

19 was rebuilt as a breakdown car in 1927 and renumbered 1.

3, 10, 11, 20, 29, 44-49 were fitted with balcony top covers in 1930.

80 was the last car to operate on the system.

APPENDIX 3 – BUS FLEET LIST

YEAR	REG Nos.	FLEET Nos.	CHASSIS	BODY	NOTES
1926	DK3443-5	1-3	Guy B	Strachan and Brown B26F	
1926	DK3446-8	4-6	Dennis E	Strachan and Brown B30D	
1926	DK3841-4	7-10	Dennis E	Strachan and Brown B30D	
1927	DK4190/1	11/2	Dennis F	Strachan and Brown B26D	
1927	DK4192-5	13-6	Dennis E	Strachan and Brown B30D	
1927-8	DK4196-8	17-9	Dennis F	Strachan and Brown B26D	
1928	DK4199	20	Dennis E	Strachan and Brown B32D	
1928	DK4682-6	21-5	Dennis E	Strachan and Brown B32D	
1928	DK5101-5	26-30	Dennis E	Strachan and Brown B32D	
1929	DK5473-7	31-5	Dennis ES	Strachan and Brown B31D	
1929	DK6208	36	Dennis EV	Strachan and Brown B31D	
1930	DK6552	37	Crossley Condor	Crossley L50R	
1930	DK6866/8	38/9	Crossley Condor	Crossley L50R	
1930	DK6865/7	40/1	Crossley Condor	Crossley L50R/	
1930	DK6871	42	Crossley Condor	Crossley L50R	
1930	DK6869	43	Crossley Condor	Crossley L50R	
1930	DK6872	44	Crossley Condor	Crossley L50R	
1930	DK6870	45	Crossley Condor	Crossley L50R	
1930	DK6876-7	46/7	Crossley Alpha	Crossley B32D	

APPENDIX 3 – BUS FLEET LIST

YEAR	REG Nos.	FLEET Nos.	CHASSIS	BODY	NOTES
1930	DK6874	48	Crossley Alpha	Crossley B32D	
1930	DK6873	49	Crossley Alpha	Crossley B32D	
1930	DK6875/8	50/1	Crossley Alpha	Crossley B32D	
1931	DK6957-9	52-4	Crossley Condor	Crossley L50R	
1931	DK6960-2	55-7	Crossley Alpha	Crossley B32D	
1931	DK7138-43	58-63	Crossley Alpha	Crossley B32D	
1931	DK7144-9	64-9	Crossley Condor	Crossley L50R	
1931	DK7480-8	70-8	Crossley Condor	Crossley H52R	
1931	DK7489-91	79-81	Dennis Lance	English Electric H52R	
1932	DK7646	82	Crossley Condor	Crossley H52R	a
1932	DK7861-72	83-94	Crossley Condor	Crossley H52R	
1932	DK7980-3	95-8	Crossley Condor	Crossley H52R	
1932	DK8014-9	99-104	Crossley Condor	Crossley H52R	
1932	DK8020-32	105-17	Crossley Condor	English Electric H52R	
1935	ADK78/9	118/9	Crossley Mancunian	MCW/Crossley H50R	
1935	ADK282/3	120/1	AEC Regent	Weymann H52R	b
1936	BDK207-10	122-5	AEC Regent	English Electric H52R	b
1936	BDK353/4	126/7	AEC Regent	Weymann H52R	
1936	BDK355/6	128/9	Leyland TD4c	Weymann H52R	
1937	CDK204-8	130-4	Leyland TS7	Cravens B35R	c
1937	CDK209-13	135-9	AEC Regent	Cravens H52R	b
1938	DDK110-4	140-4	Leyland TD5c	Cravens H54R	d
1938	DDK115-21	145-51	Leyland TD5	Eastern Coach Works H56R	
1938	DDK122-6	152-156	Daimler COG6	Cravens H54R	
1939	DDK832-6	157-61	AEC Regent	Eastern Coach Works H56R	
1939	DDK918-22	162-6	Leyland TD5	Weymann H56R	
1939	EDK101-8	6-13	Leyland TS8	Eastern Coach Works B35R	
1940	EDK645-9	167-71	Leyland TD7	English Electric H56R	
1940	EDK650-4	172-6	Leyland TD7	Eastern Coach Works H56R	
1940	EDK686-90	177-81	Daimler COG6	Eastern Coach Works H56R	
1940	EDK691-5	182-6	Daimler COG6	Eastern Coach Works H56R	e
1943	EDK771	187	Daimler CWG5	Massey H56R	
1943-4	EDK798/9	188/9	Daimler CWA6	Duple H56R	
1944	EDK800	190	Daimler CWG5	Duple H56R	
1944	EDK801/2	191-2	Daimler CWA6	Northern Counties H56R	
1944	EDK803/4	193/4	Daimler CWG5	Duple H56R	
1944	EDK805	195	Daimler CWA6	Northern Counties H56R	
1944	EDK806-9	196-9	Daimler CWG5	Northern Counties H56R	e f
1944	EDK835	200	Daimler CWG5	Duple H56R	g
1944	DDK257	130	Leyland TD5	Leyland H56R	h
1944	JD1381		AEC Regal	Beadle C32F	j
1945	EDK921-4	21/4	Daimler CWD6	Massey H56R	
1945	EDK925-30	25-30	Daimler CWA6	Massey H56R	
1947	FDK331-5	31-5	AEC Regent III	Weymann H56R	
1948	BWA212	71	AEC Regent	Weymann H56R	k
1948	CWA492	72	AEC Regent	Weymann H56R	k
1948	JX6425	73	AEC Regent	Park Royal H56R	l

APPENDIX 3 – BUS FLEET LIST

YEAR	REG Nos.	FLEET Nos.	CHASSIS	BODY	NOTES
1948	JX6568-70	74-6	AEC Regent	Roe H56R	l
1948	GDK136-48	36-48	AEC Regent III	Weymann H57R	
1948	GDK401-7	201-7	AEC Regent III	East Lancashire H57R	
1949	GDK708-22	208-22	AEC Regent III	Weymann H59R	
1950	HDK23-32	223-32	AEC Regent III	Weymann H59R	
1951	HDK701-7	301-7	AEC Regal IV	East Lancashire B42D	m
1952	HDK833-7	233-7	AEC Regent III	East Lancashire H59R	
1953	JDK708-15	308-15	AEC Regal IV	Burlingham B42D	m
1953	JDK738-52	238-52	Daimler CVG6	Weymann H59R	
1954	KDK653-67	253-67	Daimler CVG6	Weymann H59R	
1956	NDK968-97	268-97	AEC Regent V	Weymann H61R	
1956	ODK698-707	298-307	AEC Regent V	Weymann H61R	
1957	RDK408-18	308-18	AEC Regent V	Weymann H61R	
1958-9	TDK319-22	319-22	AEC Regent V	Weymann H61RD	
1961	2116-20DK	16-20	AEC Reliance	Weymann B42D	
1964	6321DK	21	AEC Reliance	East Lancashire B42D	
1964	6323-7DK	323-7	Daimler Fleetline	Weymann H77F	
1964	ADK722/3B	22/3	AEC Reliance	East Lancashire B42D	
1965	EDK128-34C	328-34	Daimler Fleetline	Weymann H77F	
1966	GDK324-9D	24-9	AEC Reliance	Willowbrook B45F	
1968	KDK135-44F	335-44	Daimler Fleetline	Metro-Cammell H77F	
1968	LDK830-3G	30-3	Daimler Fleetline	Willowbrook B45F	
1969	MDK734-7G	34-7	AEC Swift	Pennine B45F	

a 82 received the body from 106 in 1940 and was renumbered 106
b 120-5, 137 rebodied Samlesbury H57R 1951
c 130-4 renumbered 1-5 1939
d 143 rebodied Massey H57C 1946
e 198 received body of 185 1942 and renumbered 185
f 199 rebodied Rochdale Corporation H56R 1955
g 200 was a Yelloway order delivered to Rochdale
h 130 ex Yelloway, new 1938
j JD1381 ex Yelloway, new 1931
k 71, 72 new to Sheffield 1935/6
l 73-6 new to Halifax 1938
m 301-10, 312 renumbered 1-10, 12 1956 and rebuilt to B44F 1961

APPENDIX 4 – SELNEC SERVICE RENUMBERING – 1974		
ROCHDALE Number	**ROUTE**	**SELNEC Number**
1	Rochdale – Castleton via Deeplish	461
1A	Rochdale – Castleton via Oldham Road	462
3	Newhay – Rochdale – Littleborough via Entwisle Road	454
3A	Newhay – Rochdale – Littleborough via John Street	455
4A	Ashfield Road – Rochdale – Bamford via Spotland Road	444
5	Rochdale – Bamford via Bury Road	445
6	Newhay – Rochdale – Summit via Entwisle Road	454
6	Newhay – Rochdale – Stansfield via Entwisle Road	456
6A	Newhay – Rochdale – Summit via John Street	455
6A	Newhay – Rochdale – Stansfield via John Street	457
7	Healey – Rochdale – Wardle via Bentley Street and Low Hill	448
7	Healey – Rochdale – Wardle via Lowerfold and Low Hill	449
7A	Healey – Rochdale – Wardle via Bentley Street	446
7A	Healey – Rochdale – Wardle via Lowerfold	447
8	Rochdale – Middleton – Manchester express	16
8	Rochdale – Hollingworth Lake via Entwisle Road	450
8	High Peak – Littleborough – Hollingworth Lake	451
8	Shore – Littleborough – Hollingworth Lake	452
8	Calderbrook – Littleborough – Hollingworth Lake	453
9	Rochdale – Oldham – Ashton	409
9A	Rochdale – Kirkholt Flats	458
10	Syke – Rochdale – Turf Hill via Whitehall Street	440
10	Syke – Rochdale – Turf Hill via Heights Lane and Quarry Street	441
11	Rochdale – Kirkholt	463
11A	Norden – Rochdale – Kirkholt via Spotland Road	459
11C	Norden – Rochdale – Kirkholt via Mellor Street	460
12A	Rochdale – Daniel Fold – Lanehead via Spotland Road	442
14	Greave – Rochdale – Kingsway	464
15	Rochdale – Shaw	435
16	Rochdale – Bacup	465
16	Rochdale – Bacup via Mettle Cote	466
16	Rochdale – Wallbank	467
17	Rochdale – Middleton – Manchester	17
17T	Rochdale – Castleton via Tweedale Street	443
19	Rochdale – Bury via Jericho	469
21T	Rochdale – Heywood – Bury via Tweedale Street	471
24	Rochdale – Royton – Manchester	24
90	Rochdale – Royton – Manchester express	23